EXPLORING
BRIGHTON
AND THE
SOUTH DOWNS

David Harrison

S.B. Publications

By the same author:
Exploring Eastbourne and the South Downs

First published in 1996 by S.B. Publications
c/o 19 Grove Road, Seaford, East Sussex BN25 1TP

ISBN 1 85770 102 X

Typeset and printed by Island Press Ltd.
Tel: 01323 490222 UK

CONTENTS

Front Cover: Palace Pier, Brighton

Back Cover: 'Jill', the post mill at Clayton

Title Page: The Royal Pavilion

Photographs by Tony Bannister

EXPLORING BRIGHTON AND THE SOUTH DOWNS

Brighton is the best known resort in Britain. Best known for any number of reasons but it is the lesser known - indeed the unknown things perhaps that interest us just as much here. For apart from the glitter of Palace Pier, the elegance of the Grand Hotel, the majesty of the Royal Pavilion there is also the mystery of the Lanes, the intrigue of the "twittens" and the flamboyance of much of the town's architecture.

Beyond the town itself there is much to be explored; Devils Dyke, the Chattri, Jack and Jill: one a natural phenonomen, another a monument to a far off race and a unique pair of windmills, one the oldest type in existence anywhere in Britain.

Remains of an ingenious railway exist in the least expected place; the old route taken by the Brighton fishwives to sell their wares and the home of the ill fated Virginia Woolf are all included in the pages that follow.

Then there is the fishing village that with the advent of the railways became a busy port, a dream that today is a monument straddling the division of east and west hemispheres and a lost village with an eerie reminder to a past community.

All of these are included in two motor tours, routes of which are clearly outlined along with places to park and points of interest en route. Then, with the aid of 8 walks even more of this fascinating area can be explored in greater detail with simple step by step directions, instructions on points of access, a full description of everything of interest on the way along with details of toilets and refreshment facilities where available.

Details of public transport are given for those without their own transport and it is hoped with all this information it will be possible to explore even more of this fascinating part of Sussex.

BRIGHTON - A SHORT HISTORY

In Saxon times the area was held by Ulnoth, grandfather of King Harold, although there have been settlements here since Neolithic times when man preferred to live on high ground rather than the narrow strip of coastal plain where modern Brighton lies.

Around the time of Domesday 'Bristelmestune' as it was then known was a fishing community of around 90 souls and its medieval counterpart consisted of an upper part, inhabited by farmers, and a lower part where fishing families lived. It was not particularly prosperous during this period although Edward II granted it market rights in 1313.

During the sixteenth century it became vulnerable to attack and invasion during the wars with France and defences were organised but not until the town had been almost totally destroyed. Practically all of medieval Brighton was lost save for St Nicholas' church, although The Lanes give some idea what the layout would have been like.

Come the seventeenth century the local fishing industry of Brighthelmstone as it had now become known fell into decline, suffering harassment from foreign vessels and continuing competition from other British fishing fleets. Throughout the next century the sea encroached further inland and with damage done by two storms in 1703 and 1705 all the lower town was lost under mountains of shingle and even the upper town was being constantly threatened.

It was ironical, therefore, that the sea which almost destroyed Brighton should take a turn of fate to be its saviour for, following a visit from the Prince Regent one Sunday in September 1783 he was so taken by the place he bought a house there. Four years later he had a mansion built which later was transformed into the famous Pavilion and suddenly Brighton became fashionable. Elegant houses sprang up around the Pavilion and many of the squares, crescents and terraces of today belong to the Regency and Victorian era. What was once the poor fishing village of Brighthelmstone had become the most fashionable place in Sussex and the largest seaside resort in the whole of England.

Even after the death of George IV in 1830 the town's popularity remained. His successor William IV regularly stayed at the Pavilion with his wife Queen Adelaide, even making additions to it including South Lodge and Queen Adelaide's Stables, which have now been converted into the present Museum and Art Gallery. In their turn Queen Victoria and Prince Albert visited the Pavilion but with little enthusiasm. They left Brighton for the last time in February 1845 preferring the apparent tranquility of Osborne House on the Isle of Wight.

By this time the railway between London and Brighton had opened bringing with it day trippers which heralded the start of a tourist phenomenon that reached its height in the 1860's, not entirely a welcome development for Brighton was no longer considered a select watering place but a seaside town with all the amusements needed to cater for the masses.

There followed a period of depression at the turn of the century when the upper classes virtually deserted the resort but with Edward VII making regular visits the town suddenly became fashionable again.

With the onset of the First World War Brighton became a haven from the air raids on London and the Pavilion was used as a hospital for Indian soldiers with over 4000 being treated there by April 1916. Come the Second World War and the threat of invasion visitors were banned from the town and the piers were breached. It took on an eerie deserted air that remained throughout hostilities but following the armistice in 1945 a rigorous rebuilding programme began and it became the home for many London commuters.

In 1961 The University of Brighton was granted its charter becoming the first of Britain's post-war universities. By 1990 it had over 5000 students many of them renting rooms in accommodation that once catered for the influx of holidaymakers in its tourist heyday.

It is apparent that Brighton has always adapted well to its new concepts while at the same time retaining its unique charm that have rightly christened it 'The Queen of Watering places'.

BRIGHTON - A TOWN WALK

A walking tour of the town in the best way to appreciate all the major delights of this resort beginning from the Palace Pier, the second most visited attraction in Britain after Blackpool's Pleasure Beach.

1. *Turn right from Palace Pier* **(A)** *along Madeira Drive to Volk's Electric Railway* **(B)**. *Continue a further 150 yards (140m) to the Athina B Anchor* **(C)**.

2. *Return to the Sea Life Centre* **(D)** *then back to Palace Pier crossing the road opposite Royal Albion Hotel before following the pavement round to Old Steine* **(E)**. *Continue along to the YMCA which was Mrs Fitzherbert's House* **(F)**.

3. *Turn left up Steine Lane then left and right into The Lanes* **(G)** *past English's famous Oyster Bar* **(H)**. *Turn right into Brighton Place then left into Meeting House Lane opposite the original House of Correction built in the reign of William IV in 1835.*

4. *Turn left at the Friends Centre then immediately past the Cricketers* **(I)** *turn right along Black Lion Lane* **(J)** *continuing straight across into Ship Street Gardens passing Fig Tree Cottage on the left.*

5. *Turn right past the old Hippodrome (now Mecca Bingo) into Middle Street* **(K)** *following this round right before turning right into Ship Street then left into Union Street and turning left at the Font and Firkin public house built in 1688.*

6. *Cross North Street into New Road turning right into Pavilion Gardens and the Royal Pavilion* **(L)**. *Opposite is the Dome* **(M)** *then continue through the impressive Indian Memorial Gateway set up by the Indian Princes in gratitude for the hospitality of Brighton to the Indian soldiers during the Great War before turning left into Church Street past the Museum and Art Gallery* **(N)** *and Public Library.*

7. *Continue past the Corn Exchange* **(P)** *turning right along Gardner Street and ahead at Kensington Gardens into North Laines. Turn left into Gloucester Road as far as the Pond public house below which is a delightful row of old cottages along Frederick Gardens.*

8. *Turn down Trafalgar Terrace where the gardens on the right belong to the cottages on the left, then left into Trafalgar Street to the Sussex Toy and Model Museum* **(R)**.

9. *Continue up the hill to Brighton Station* **(S)**. *Proceed up Guildford Road taking the first turning left (before Guildford Street) along Camden Terrace past some original weather-boarded cottages. Turn left then right along North Gardens then ahead along Crown Gardens to Church Street where turn right for the Parish Church of St Nicholas* **(T)**.

BRIGHTON – A TOWN WALK

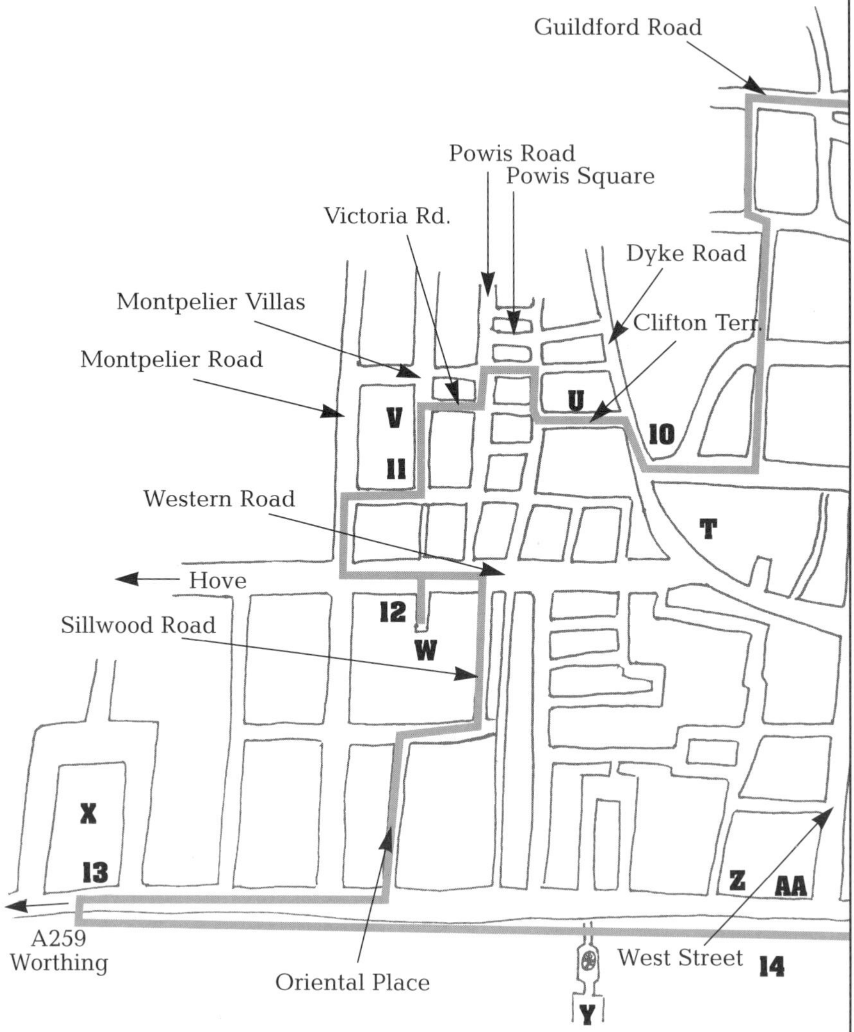

Guildford Road

Powis Road
Powis Square

Victoria Rd.

Dyke Road

Montpelier Villas

Clifton Terr.

Montpelier Road

V
11

U

10

Western Road

T

Hove

12
W

Sillwood Road

X
13

Z **AA**

A259
Worthing

Oriental Place

West Street **14**

Y

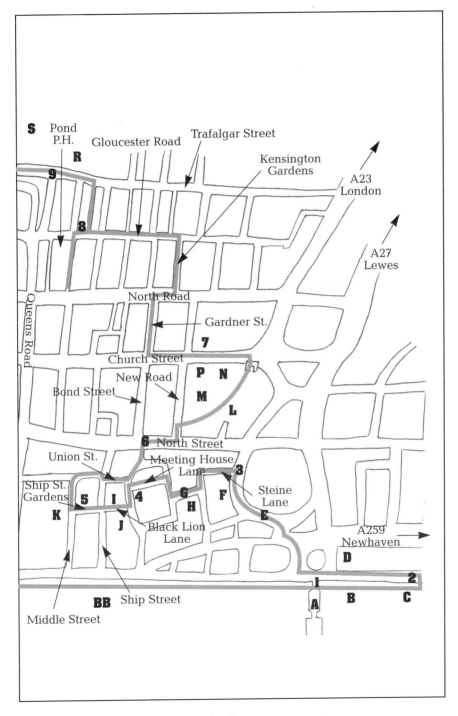

S Pond
P.H.
R
Gloucester Road
Trafalgar Street
Kensington
Gardens
A23
London
9
8
A27
Lewes
North Road
Gardner St.
7
Church Street
New Road
P N
Bond Street
M
L
Union St.
6 North Street
Meeting House
Lane
3
Ship St.
Gardens
5 I 4 G F
Steine
Lane
K
H
E
J
Black Lion
Lane
A259
Newhaven
D
2
I
BB Ship Street
B C
Middle Street
A

Queens Road

10. *Turn left into Clifton Terrace* **(U)** *then right into Powis Villas taking the first left into Powis Square and left again into Powis Road. Turn right into Victoria Road then left along Montpelier Villas* **(V)**.

11. *At the T-junction turn right then left at the traffic lights into Montpelier Road. Cross Western Road then turn left along it turning first right immediately past Debenhams into Western Terrace to the Western Pavilion* **(W)**.

12. *Return to Western Road and turn right turning right again at Sillwood Road. Turn right at the end of Sillwood Road then left down Oriental Place to the seafront where turn right into Hove.*

13. *Cross the road opposite Brunswick Square* **(X)** *returning along the promenade to West Pier* **(Y)**. *Further on above the children's paddling pool are the impressive Metropole and Grand Hotel* **(Z)** *next to the Brighton Centre* **(AA)**.

14.*Continue to the Brighton Fishing Museum* **(BB)** *then on to Palace Pier to conclude the walk.*

PLACES OF INTEREST

(A) PALACE PIER

It is the younger of the town's two piers started in 1891 but not completed until 1899, 33 years after West Pier. It was an immediate success with visitors and has remained so ever since, thought by many

Palace Pier.

to be the finest pier ever built. It was breached during World War II as a defensive measure and has been added to and improved over the years. Today it houses the National Museum of Penny Slot Machines and is packed with machines and gadgets to provide endless hours of fun for its many visitors each year.

Open all year daily. Free admission. Telephone: 01273 609361.

(B) VOLK'S RAILWAY

Opened in 1883 it was the first regular electric train service in Britain, a 1¹/₂mile (2.5km) sea-front railway taking passengers to Black Rock and the new 120 acre Marina, the largest in Europe. It was the brainchild of Magnus Volk, a local man, who was also the first person to install domestic electric light and a telephone system in the town. The railway originally ran to Rottingdean mounted on stilts to evade the tide, but this stretch had to close to make way for groynes to prevent cliff erosion. There is a stop half way at Peter Pan's Playground.

Open daily March-September (Weedays 11-5, weekends and Bank Holidays 10.30-6). Single fares payable per journey. Telephone: 01273 681061.

Volk's Electric Railway.

(C) ATHINA B ANCHOR

The Athina B was beached in a storm during the night of 21st January 1980. All her crew were successfully taken off without loss of life thanks to the bravery of the Shoreham Lifeboat and her cargo was discharged.

It took almost a month to refloat her and the anchor was presented to the town when she was finally broken up later the same year.

Free access all year.

(D) SEA LIFE CENTRE

Incorporating an aquarium now more than 100 years old one of the tanks contains 100,000 gallons of sea water and exhibits include everything from shrimps to sharks, starfish to stingrays, octopus and conger eel.

Open every day (except Christmas Day) from 10-5 (closes 6pm during the summer months). Admission charge. Telephone: 01273 604233.

(E) OLD STEINE

Steine is a Scandinavian word for a large stone and this was formerly common land where fishermen dried their nets and beached their boats during a storm. It became the promenade of fashionable folk with its spacious gardens and statues of George IV and Queen Victoria.

Old Steine.

(F) MRS FITZHERBERT'S HOUSE

The YMCA hostel on the left is the old Steine House or House of Mrs Fitzherbert, morganatic wife of George IV. Although she had a drawing room in the Royal Pavilion she never actually lived there. Because of her lack of blue blood, two previous marriages and her Catholic faith, her marriage to the Prince Regent in 1785 was always officially denied. She lived discreetly in her own house here which was built for her in 1804 and she died here in 1837. The YMCA refronted the building in 1884 obliterating most of the original exterior but most of the interior remains unchanged including a cast-iron imitation bamboo staircase matching a similar one in the Royal Pavilion. According to legend a secret underground passage connects the house to the Pavilion but in fact there is only one underground passage from the Pavilion, that connecting it to the Dome.

External viewing only.

Y.M.C.A., formerly Mrs Fitzherbert's house.

(G) THE LANES

This was the centre of medieval Brighton, formerly a series of ill-lit narrow alleyways known as "twittens". Today it is a lively, bustling area

Market Street.

full of antique shops, jewellers, craft shops and fashionable boutiques. They give the impression of something like what the old town would have been like but in fact most of the buildings date back only to the nineteenth century.

The Lanes.

(H) ENGLISH'S OYSTER BAR

In Edwardian days it was called Cheeseman's Oyster Bar and run by two sisters who banned smoking on the premises for fear of impairing the flavour of the oysters. When one day Edward VII entered the restaurant smoking a cigar the sisters refused to serve him until the offending weed was extinguished, which he did without protest.

Open normal trading hours. Telephone: 01273 327980.

(I) CRICKETERS ARMS

It was originally called The Last and Fish Cart, a last being equivalent to 10,000 fish. It changed its name to the Cricketers in the 1790's when it was a popular coaching inn for the landlord, Mr Jutton, was a keen cricket enthusiast. Next door is the inn yard the last site of the town pound which was still used as such until the 1860's.

Open normal trading hours. Telephone: 01273 329472.

(J) BLACK LION LANE

One of the narrowest of the Lanes and the topic of two favourite local stories emphasising the fact. One concerns an obese gentleman who challenged a notable athlete to a race with the condition that he could choose the course and would be allowed a 10 yard start. His conditions were accepted and he chose Black Lion Lane scoring an easy victory for there was no room for his oponent to overtake him! It is also said to have been involved in Charles II's escape from Brighton. Being carried down the Lane on the back of a fisherman they encountered a fishwife with no room to pass. Afraid to go back the fisherman knocked the woman down and clambered over her in order to take his Royal passenger to safety.

(K) MIDDLE STREET

East Street, Middle Street, West Street and North Street are the survivors of the original Tudor rectangular layout of Brighton. The area between Middle Street and East Street was known as the Hempshares, a place where hemp was grown for the fishermen's nets.

(L) ROYAL PAVILION

Built by John Nash of Regent Street for George, Prince Regent, the large dome rises 130 feet (39.6m) and the front is 375 feet (114.3m) long. Its rooms are decorated with oriental splendour and under the dome is the rotunda. The music room is lavishly decorated in Chinese style with dragons and serpents at the windows, on the walls and round the gilded columns. The walls are covered in Chinese scenes on a crimson

Entrance to the Royal Pavilion.

backdrop; the artist who spent two years painting them died a pauper in Islington workhouse. A Chinese gallery 160 feet (48.75m) long has Chinese lanterns from Buckingham Palace while the banqueting room has a shining chandelier of glass and dazzling stone which hung in Buckingham Palace in the Victorian era.

Open daily (except Christmas Day and Boxing Day) 10-6 (closes 5pm during October-May). Admission charge. Telephone: 01273 603005.

(M) THE DOME

Built 1803-5 as the stables and riding school for the Pavilion it takes its name from its enormous central cupola measuring 85 feet (25.9m) across and 65 feet (19.8m) high. Its architect, William Porden, drew his inspiration from the Paris Cornmarket and the Great Mosque in Delhi. Forty horses were housed here in stalls in a great circle with a pool and fountain for watering them in the centre. In the balcony were harness rooms and accommodation for the grooms and coachmen. Today it is used for concerts and conferences with seating for over 2000.

Box Office Telephone: 01273 709709

The Dome.

(N) MUSEUM AND ART GALLERY

This is also housed in part of the former stable complex, containing old masters and exhibits of pottery, primitive art and local natural history. Brighton's early history is well illustrated here and the ethnographic displays - the best in England after London - should not be missed. The adjoining library has been enriched by gifts from many private collections.

Free admission. Open 10-5 (2-5 Sundays) throughout the year but closed Wednesdays, New Years Day, Good Friday, Christmas Day and Boxing Day. Telephone: 01273 603005

Museum, Art Gallery and Library.

(P) CORN EXHANGE

Behind the Dome the old Riding House where the Prince Regent used to exercise his horses became the Corn Exhcange in the late nineteenth centruy and is now an exhibition hall.

Telephone: 01273 674357.

Kensington Gardens.

(R) SUSSEX TOY AND MODEL MUSEUM

Situated in Trafalgar Street underneath the arches at Brighton Railway Station the Museum houses a priceless toy and model train collection, scale model aeroplanes, dolls and dolls houses, Meccano, jigsaws and puzzles, model cars, lorries and buses, ships of all shapes and sizes and many more toys and models from all over the world.

Admission charge. Open daily 10-5 (11-5 Sundays and Bank Holidays). Telephone: 01273 749494.

(S) BRIGHTON RAILWAY STATION

Originally called Central Station it was designed by David Macotta in 1840 in classical Italian style. Nine graceful arches with slender pilars gave it a sense of elegance while its Venetian grand entrance gave it a feeling of imporatnce. The first train to leave its platforms departed 21st September 1841 for London Bridge. In 1882 the roof was raised but the Gothic archways and iron columns remained supporting 3000 large panes of glass. Today the station is almost unchanged in over 150 years.

Telephone: 01273 206755

(T) ST NICHOLAS' CHURCH

Built in the fourteenth century the church contains a splendidly carved Norman font, an exquisite piece of Caen stone which most probably came from the Cluniac Priory at Lewes. The scenes depicted on it include the

St Nicholas' Church.

Last Supper, the Baptism of Christ and episodes from the life of St Nicholas. Also inside are several tombs and monuments and an interesting memorial to the Duke of Wellington who went to school in Brighton. The painted roof of the chancel with its gilded bosses is hard to see in the gloom of the interior as is the fourteenth century screen, carved and painted as fine as any in the county. In the churchyard are the remains of three local celebrities; Captain Nicholas Tettersal who took Charles II to the safety of France after the Battle of Worcester in 1651: Phoebe Hassell, who was 108 when she died in 1821, and hers is an extraordinary story for in her youth she disguised herself as a boy and joined the British Army to be near her solider lover who had been posted to the West Indies. She served undetected for seventeen years until being wounded at the Battle of Fonteroy when she disclosed her secret to the regimental Colonel's wife; and finally Martha Gunn, 'Queen of the Dippers', attendants who looked after women bathers in the eighteenth century.

(U) CLIFTON TERRACE

Built in 1850 after the death of George IV and one of the many Victorian developments that contains almost as many buildings of the Regency style that were built in Regency Square at the time when the Prince Regent lived in the town.

(V) MONTPELIER VILLAS

Designed in 1845 by Amon Henry Wilds who built a host of houses in various styles in the town. These were arguably his finest work built towards the end of an illustrious career with their bold eaves and projecting, canopied bow windows typical of his later style. The ammonite motif, a pun on his name, is noticably missing on this occasion. *External view only.*

(W) WESTERN PAVILION

A miniature version of the Royal Pavilion this too was built by Amon Henry Wilds and was his home for several years from 1833. The Gothic House opposite was designed in 1822 by his father who with Charles Busby was also reponsible for much of the finest housing schemes in Regency Brighton. *External view only.*

(X) BRUNSWICK SQUARE

Along with Brunswick Terrace this was a speculative development built on open farmland between 1824/8 and inspired by the Nash terraces of Regents Park. It was the work of Amon Wilds senior and Charles Busby whose style of massive neoclassical facades and bow fronts are evident here.

(Y) WEST PIER

Completed in 1866 by Eugenius Birch this was without doubt the finest pier ever built. Based on the Royal Pavilion many of its original cast iron supporting columns are still in sound condition even after 130 years and plans are afoot to restore the pier to its former glory by the end of the century. In 1893 the pier head was widened and the large pavilion was built which served as a theatre until the outbreak of the Second World War. The concert hall halfway down the pier was added in 1916 and continued to function until it bacame a casualty of war. The Pier was returned to public use after the war but by 1975 its condition had deteriated so badly it was closed and left sadly neglected. It is however a Grade I listed building, the only pier to be so, and therefore unique in more ways than one.

(Z) GRAND HOTEL

The Grand Hotel was opened in 1864 with its nine stories and 260 rooms and was one of the first hotels in England to be fitted with electric light and lifts. It fell into disrepair in the 1960's but was restored to its former Victorian glory only to be destroyed by a bomb intended to decimate the Conservative cabinet in 1984 as it gathered for the Party conference. Again it was lovingly restored and it remains one of the country's leading hotels today.
   Telephone: 01273 321188.

The Metropole and Grand Hotels with the Brighton Centre on the right.

(AA) BRIGHTON CENTRE

Almost next door to the Grand is the Brighton Centre built at a cost of over £9m and opened in 1977 as the premier conference centre in Britain. Its versatility provides facilities for a wide variety of functions: its huge main hall seats up to 5,120 while the smaller Hewison Hall holds 800 and the new East Wing 600 in each of its two rooms. Beyond is **The Old Ship Inn**, the oldest inn in Brighton. The earliest reference to it dates back to 1559 but its origins are believed to go back much further. During the eighteenth century it became the social centre of the town when Ship Street was one of the main thoroughfares. The Assembly Rooms added in 1775 were used for important town and business meetings as well as social functions and still remains one of the leading hotels in the resort.

Telephone: 01273 202881.

(BB) FISHING MUSEUM

A recent addition to the Seafront situated underneath the arches below Ship Street.

For further information and details of opening times Telephone: 01273 723064.

The Brighton Fishing Museum.

OTHER PLACES OF INTEREST

1. The British Engineerium

Situated in Woodland Drive, Hove in a beautifully restored nineteenth century water pumping station which now houses hundreds of model engines plus full size traction and fire engines from yesteryear. *Open daily 10-5pm. Telephone: 01273 559583.*

2. Preston Manor

Situated about two miles north of Brighton on the A23 London road Preston Manor was an old Manor House built about 1250, rebuilt in 1738 and substantially added to and altered in 1905. It was bought by the Stanford family in 1794 and for 138 years was their family home. In 1932 the house and its contents were left to Brighton Borough Council and in 1988 extensive restorations presented a unique opportunity to show both "upstairs" and "downstairs" of an Edwardian home.

Open all year from Tuesday-Saturday 10-5pm and Sunday 2-5pm. Closed on Monday (except Bank Holidays), Good Friday, Christmas Day and Boxing Day. Telephone: 01273 713239.

3. King Alfred Leisure Centre

On the seafront in Hove it is one of the most popular leisure centres in the south-east with its three pools, water slides, ten pin bowling, snooker, badminton and indoor bowls as well as fully equipped fitness centre. *Telephone: 01273 822228.*

4. Prince Regent Swimming Complex

In the heart of Brighton town centre complete with swimming pools, fitness area, solarium and sauna. *Telephone: 01273 685692.*

5. Pirate's Deep Children's Play Centre

An indoor children's play centre including Smugglers' Tavern, multi-activity soft play area, ball pools, tube slides etc. Fully supervised. *Admission charge (accompanying adults free). Open daily during summer months 11-4.45pm and at weekends and school holidays during the winter. Telephone: 01273 674549.*

MOTOR TOUR – ONE

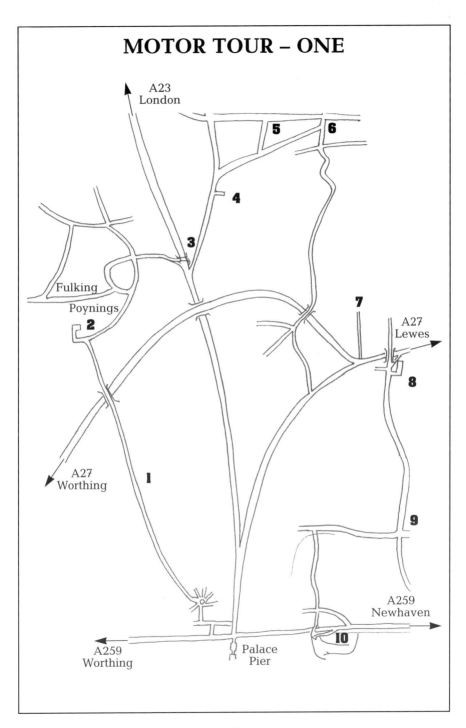

MOTOR TOUR – ONE (37½ miles/60km)

BRIGHTON – BOOTH MUSEUM OF NATURAL HISTORY
DEVIL'S DYKE – PYECOMBE – CLAYTON WINDMILLS
KEYMER – DITCHLING – STANMER PARK – FALMER
WOODINGDEAN – MARINA – BRIGHTON

1. Palace Pier – Booth Museum of Natural History (2 miles/3.2km)

Leave Palace Pier westward along Grand Junction Road towards West Pier. In ³/₄mile (1.2km) turn right into Preston Street at the traffic lights by West Beach Hotel then left into Western Road. At the next traffic lights turn right into Montpelier Road taking the second left at Seven Dials signposted Devils Dyke. In 2 miles (3.2km) reach the Booth Museum of Natural History where there is ample roadside parking alongside the park.

2. Booth Museum of Natural History – Devil's Dyke (4½ miles/7.2km)

Continue ahead along Dyke Road to a roundabout in about 2¼ miles (3.6km) where bear left signposted Devil's Dyke. Follow all signs for Devil's Dyke which reach in a further 2¼ miles (3.6km) where there is car parking available.

3. Devil's Dyke – Pyecombe (9 miles/14.5km)

Return to the junction in ½ mile (0.8km) and turn left signposted Poynings. In a further mile (1.6km) turn left at the T-junction at Saddlescombe Road and in another ½ mile (0.8km) take an obtuse turn left signposted Poynings. Turn left in ¼ mile (0.4km) signposted Fulking by the church in Poynings (see page 54) (where there is very limited parking) and in 1½ miles (2.4km) reach the Shepherd and Dog Public House in Fulking to view the spring (see page 53). Retrace route ¼ mile (0.4km) to bear left at Clapper Lane, turning right at the T-junction in 1³/₄ miles (2.8km) signposted Brighton and follow the signs A281 and A23 for Brighton. In another 3 miles (4.8km) turn off left at the A273 signposted Pyecombe where there is unlimited parking by the roadside near the Plough Inn.

4. Pyecombe – Clayton Windmills (1¼ miles/2km)

Turn left onto the A273 signposted Hassocks. In ³/₄ mile (1.2km) turn right at Mill Lane signposted Windmill where the car park is ½ mile (0.8km) further along on the left.

5. Clayton Windmills – Keymer (2¹/₂ miles/4km)

Return to A273 and turn right, turning right again signposted Ditchling. In a further mile (1.6km) turn left signposted Keymer, turning right at the T-junction in the village where there is limited parking in The Crescent, first turning left after the church.

6. Keymer – Ditchling (³/₄ mile/1.2km)

Follow The Crescent round right turning left back onto the B2116 to Ditchling where there is ample parking off left beside the pond immediately before the church.

7. Ditchling – Stanmer Park (8¹/₂ miles/13.7km)

Return to the B2116 turning left. Turn right at the crossroads onto the B2112 keeping straight ahead over Ditchling Beacon. At the T-junction turn left following the signs for Coldean and Stanmer Park. Turn left at the traffic lights onto the A27 then left again onto the slip road into Stanmer Park where there is a car park round right by the church.

8. Stanmer Park – Falmer (2¹/₂ miles/4km)

Return to the A27 keeping to the nearside lane signposted Rottingdean/Falmer. Turn right at the roundabout over the A27 keeping straight ahead past the slip road to Brighton before taking the next on the left signposted Falmer South where there is unlimited parking round the pond.

9. Falmer – Woodingdean (1¹/₂ miles/2.4km)

Turn left back onto the B2123 and in 1¹/₂ miles (2.4km) left onto a parking area immediately before the Sunblest Bakery.

10. Woodingdean – Marina (3 miles/4.8km)

Turn left back onto the B2123 then right at the traffic lights by the Downs Hotel signposted Marina/Town Centre. Turn left at Wilson Avenue over the racecourse keeping ahead at the traffic lights and following the signs for Marina. Turn sharp left at the roundabout for parking in the large Asda car park.

11. Marina – Palace Pier (2 miles/3.2km)

Right round the roundabout out of the car park keeping to the offside lane for Brighton. In ³/₄ mile (1.2km) bear left down Dukes Mound then ahead back to Palace Pier.

POINTS OF INTEREST DURING THE TOUR

1. Booth Museum of Natural History

The Museum was built in 1874 to house E.T. Booth's fantastic collection of British birds mounted in detailed settings creating their natural environments, with over 500 individual displays. A gallery displaying animal skeletons rare and extinct is also on view with pride of place taken by the skeleton of a large killer whale. Three other galleries deal with man's effects on the environment, showing the importance of conservation; another shows butterflies from all over the world and a third displays a selection of local chalk fossils, flint and minerals and the Iguanadon, a local dinosaur.

Access for wheelchairs may be made by prior arrangement. A Museum shop is available and the Museum has Free Admission.

Hours of Opening: Open all year 10-5 weekdays (except Thurs) 2-5 Sundays. Closed Good Friday, Christmas Day, Boxing Day and New Years Day. Telephone: (01273) 552586.

Public Transport: Services 10 and 11 operated by Brighton Blue Buses from Old Steine pass the Museum every 15 minutes during the week and every 30 minutes on Sunday.

Booth Museum of Natural History.

2. Devil's Dyke

One of the best known and most written about parts of Sussex Devil's Dyke, along with most other natural phenomena, is attributed to the work of the Devil although it is more likely a combe made during the melting of the Ice Age. Local legend has it that Satan, being concerned by the increasing number of churches being built in the Weald, decided to put a stop to the popular Christian beliefs by digging a dyke through the Downs so that the next high tide would breach his defence and so flood the low-lying land beyond. Disturbed by his labour an old lady ventured outside with a lantern to see what all the fuss was about and seeing the light and thinking it daybreak the Devil threw the last shovel full of earth over his shoulder forming the Isle of Wight before deserting his task leaving the Dyke unfinished as we see it today.

A curved valley some ³/₄ mile (1.2km) in length and 700 feet (215m) high it does indeed look like an artificial excavation and to give the legend even more authenticity when, in the early part of the twentieth century a railway line was built from Brighton, the skeleton of a woman was uncovered by digging navvies who was immediately believed to be the one who thwarted the Devil's labours all those centuries earlier.

The promontory formed between the Dyke and the escarpment made it an obvious choice for an Iron Age hill fort, ramparts of which can still be seen stretching across the neck of the promontory near the car park. There are magnificent views from the car park overlooking the Weald

Devil's Dyke.

and this has been a popular tourist attraction for over 200 years. The first hotel was built here in 1817 and it was a subsequent landlord who boosted its popularity by building the railway up the side of the Downs.

Public Transport: Access to the Dyke is either by car or on foot for today there is no public transport serving the area.

Walk: A circular walk 5¹/₂ miles (8.8km) including some splendid downland scenery and incorporating the villages of Fulking and Poynings begins from the car park (see page 49).

Toilets and Refreshments available at the Dyke Hotel.

3. Pyecombe

It became famous in the nineteenth century for producing shepherd's crooks. A Mr Berry seems to have developed the particular Pyecombe style around 1820 although his method of manufacture appears to have been kept a secret. A later manufacturer, Charles Mitchell, developed the craft for around sixty years, receiving orders from as far away as New Zealand.

Apparently the best crooks were made from old gun barrels with the staves of ash or hazel. The end of the crook, which is curled to avoid becoming a sharp point, is known as the 'guide', which on all Pyecombe crooks is always longer than on any other. Today the only existing specimens are found mainly in museums.

Tapsell gate with shepherd's crook gate latch, Pyecombe.

The gate latch to the church is even made out of the curved iron top of a shepherd's crook and was actually produced in the building opposite, for the single-storey extension to the house was once a forge specialising in the manufacture of crooks.

The church of this tiny hamlet has as its prize possession one of only three lead fonts in Sussex and one of the largest specimens in England, with fine Norman lead work dating from around 1170. It also has a rare triple chancel arch, the centre arch being Norman and very beautiful, an East window glowing in rich colours which seem to stand out in the contrasting darkness of the chancel and some thirteenth century tiles by the altar. Unfortunately in keeping with a sign of the time with all these treasures within the church is generally kept locked.

Public Transport: Service 107 Brighton-Horsham operates hourly Monday to Saturday and two-hourly on Sundays. Service 770 Brighton-Haywards Heath operates half-hourly Monday to Saturday with NO service on Sunday.

Toilets and refreshments available at the Plough Inn.

4. Clayton Windmills
Known affectionately as 'Jack and Jill', the former is a brick tower mill while the latter is a white painted post mill.

Jill, the older of the two, was originally built in 1821 in Dyke Road, Brighton, and was subsequently moved to its present site although

Jack and Jill Windmills, Clayton.

when remains a bit of a mystery. Jack was built in 1866 and Jill was re-erected beside it when both mills were worked by James Mitchell, a local farmer.

Jack ceased working in 1908 followed by Jill the following year. Then, during a storm in 1909, Jack lost two sails and his fantail and the remaining two sails were subsequently removed.

Henry Longhurst, golfing correspondent of the Sunday Times, later owned the mills handing over the care of Jill to Cuckfield Rural District Council in 1958. Eight years later agreement was reached between Mr Longhurst, East Sussex District Council and Cuckfield Rural District Council over the future maintenance of Jack and in 1973 he was restored to something like his former glory by Universal Pictures who required both mills for a film sequence in *The Black Windmill* spending £3,000 on the fitting of four new sails.

There is a Jack and Jill Preservation Society and it is hoped to return Jill to full working order and to turn Jack into a museum of Sussex mills and milling. Whatever their fate it is important the mills survive for they are good examples of the two distinct windmill types – the brick built tower mill and the wooden post mill, the latter being the earliest type of windmill built in England.

Public Transport: Service 770 Brighton - Haywards Heath operates every 30 minutes Mondays to Saturdays with NO service on Sundays. The windmills are situated ¹/₂ mile (0.8km) from the A273 along Mill Lane at Clayton.

Walk: A 6 mile (9.6km) circuit begins from the car park along part of the South Downs Way to Pyecombe then up Wolstonbury Hill returning through Clayton. (see page 55).

5. Keymer

Domesday Book records a church at 'Chemer' although the oldest part of the existing church dates back no further than the 13th century; the chancel with an apse and a painted and gilded roof. Most seen today is later than 1866 when the whole church was rebuilt, albeit in the style of the original. Unfortunately wall paintings in the chancel were lost during this transformation.

The church is dedicated to Saints Cosmas and Damian two Syrian medical missionaries who happened to be brothers and suffered martyrdom in the 4th Century. They are the patron saints of doctors and dedications to them are rare for there are no more than five churches in the whole of England sharing a similar dedication.

Stanmer Church.

To the older residents the village is still called Kymer though most now recognise it in its more traditional name of Keymer. The Manor has been held at least in part by most of the great families over the centuries, with records showing the de Warennes, the Duke of Norfolk, the Earl of Derby, the Goring family and the Nevills (who were Lords Bergavenny, later adding the A that made them the familiar Abergavenny's) all having owned it at some time in history.

Along Lodge Lane is Oldlands Post Mill which is thought to have been built in the 17th century although it last worked as long ago as 1918. In 1927 it came under the care of the Sussex Archaeological Society and it is currently undergoing a restoration programme.

The Keymer Brick and Tile Company was established in 1875 by Samuel Copestake and its handmade tiles and bricks have been used in many well known buildings throughout the nation.

Toilets and refreshments are available in the village.

Public Transport: There is no direct service from Brighton to Keymer by bus. A minimal service operates from Lewes with rail connections from Brighton but it is advisable to seek advice before travelling.

6. Ditchling

The Manor of Ditchling was once the property of King Alfred and later belonged to Edward the Confessor. Edward II kept a stud of horses here when he was Prince of Wales for hunting in the royal park and in 1312 he granted permission for a market to be held each Tuesday.

With its superb setting in the shadow of Ditchling Beacon it is a quaint old place with lovely timbered cottages highlighted with Wings Place opposite the parish church. Legend has it this 500 year old property was given to Anne of Cleves by Henry VIII although it is a matter for speculation whether she ever actually lived there. More likely is the belief that when put up for auction in 1894 the Victorian vendors 'created' royal association with the property in order to attain a better sale.

The 13th Century parish church of St Margaret is kept locked which is a great pity for inside are three stone coffin lids 600 years old; the old pitch pipe with which the choir was given the note before the luxury of an organ and a chest as old as the church itself.

From the churchyard the **Ditchling Museum** is housed in adjacent buildings that served as the village school for 150 years. Displays include dioramas and costume tableaux together with country crafts, farm implements and Chamber of Horrors.

Hours of Opening: Monday-Saturday 11-5, Sundays 2-5 (Open weekends only in winter until 4.30pm) Church Lane, Ditchling. Tel: 01273 844744.

Other places of interest in the village include The Craftsman Gallery and Jill Pryke Pottery in the High Street, displaying a large variety of Sussex crafts: pottery, wood turning, corn dollies, candles and jewellery. (Open Monday-Saturday 10-5 closed Wednesday, Tel: 01273 845246)

The Ditchling Gallery housed in a 17th Century low-beamed cottage in the High Street holds changing exhibitions amid a collection of etchings, engravings and artists paraphernalia including picture framing. (Open Tuesday-Saturday 10.30-5pm but closed 1-2.30pm and Wednesday afternoon. Tel: 01273 843342).

A little way out of the village is Stoneywish Country Park with its tea rooms, pets corner and children's play area. Open every day in the summer 10-7pm (last admission 5pm) November-February open 10-5pm (last admission 3pm) Tel: 01273 843408.

Public Transport: There is no direct service to Ditchling from Brighton by bus. A minimal service operates from Lewes with rail connections from Brighton but it is advisable to seek advice before travelling.

7. Stanmer Park

The name Stanmer is derived from the Saxon 'staen mere' meaning stony pond. It is widely believed that the pond beside the parish church gave Stanmer its name and the 18th Century Palladian mansion Stanmer Place opposite was once the home of the Pelham family, Earls of Chichester. The Pelhams acquired the estate in 1714 and apart from building the large country house they also landscaped the park and woodlands.

Falmer Church.

The tiny village was evacuated during the Second World War and taken over by the army who used it as a mock battlefield inflicting much damage. Now it is owned by Brighton Borough Council who have restored it to its former condition, save for the mansion which is in a sorry state. Behind it the local Preservation Society have installed a small Rural Museum which is open from time to time with free admission.

The church belongs to the last century and owes much to the Pelhams. In the nave is a monument to Sir John Pelham kneeling in Elizabethan armour at a desk with his wife, their young son beside them. Death struck the Earl who was soon followed by his son. Earlier this century the sixth Earl of Chichester died at Stanmer Park and was succeeded by his son who eight days later had died too. The strange re-occurrence of this tragedy is all the more poignant by the fact that they laid them both to rest in this place.

Walk: A superb circular walk begins from the church to Ditchling Beacon, the second highest point on the South Downs and offers an opportunity to visit the Chattri, a mysterious Indian monument, before returning through the splendid Stanmer parkland. (8¹/₂ miles/14km) (see page 59)
Toilets and refreshments available. Ideal for picnics.

Public Transport: Service 25,28 and 729 operated by Brighton and Hove/Stagecoach at 20, 15 and 60 minute intervals accordingly for Brighton University. Foot access to the Park at all times. On Sundays service 25 does not operate and services 28 and 729 are every 2 hours.

8. Falmer

A divided village today, not socially but physically. The building of the busy A27 was responsible, cutting the old community in two, but a pedestrian bridge has helped span the divide and life goes on much the same.

The building of Brighton Polytechnic and Sussex University on the doorstep of the village has brought even more change to what was once a rural life but the blissful tranquillity of the village pond has virtually remained unchanged. It was the pond, once sixteen feet deep until part of it was filled in, that gave the village its name; Faelmere eventually becoming Falmer.

The church is relatively modern to most in the area and is generally kept locked.

The journalist Godfrey Winn, who had a regular column in the Daily Mirror for many years, lived in Mill House and died here in 1971.

Refreshments and toilet facilities at the Swan Inn.

Public Transport: Service 25, 28 and 729 operated by Brighton and Hove/Stagecoach every 20,15 and 60 minutes accordingly. Alight at University. Service 25 does not operate on Sunday and services 28 and 729 operate every 2 hours.

9. Woodingdean

On the face of things here is just an urban development that is rapidly becoming a Brighton overspill but it does have its own identity – and unique claim to fame!

In 1839 it originated as part of the now lost hamlet of Balsdean (see page 79) although then it was known as Woodendean, not changing to its present name until the early 1920's. By 1930 the population had grown sufficiently to support a number of shops and other facilities situated around the crossroads where the Downs Hotel stands today. By the mid-sixties the population had risen to over 9,000.

Errol Flynn's parents lived in the village and he often came to visit them whenever his filming commitments permitted until his mother was tragically killed while crossing the Falmer road in 1966.

As to its claim to fame Woodingdean Well at 1285 feet (391.67m) is the deepest hand dug well in Great Britain. With work commencing on the 22nd March 1858 it took 45 men four years to dig and consists of two shafts the first connected to the second by means of a heading or tunnel. Its combined depth is equal in height to the Empire State Building and is brick lined in its entirety. On completion it contained 200,000 gallons of pure water. It still exists today but has been capped off for safety reasons.

Toilet and refreshments available.

Public Transport: Service 2, 22 operated by Brighton and Hove Buses every 20 or 15 minutes (hourly on Sunday) or service 52A operated by Brighton Blue Bus/Local Rider every 60 minutes with NO service on Sunday.

10. Marina

Opened by H.M. Queen Elizabeth II in May 1979 the massive harbour walls enveloping 77 acres of sheltered water offering moorings for 2,000

Brighton Marina.

craft made it the largest marina in Europe. Its village complex contains sports shops, galleries, boutiques, pubs, restaurants and residential area built around an inner lagoon. Other entertainments apart from fishing include Fast-Trax speed karting and an eight-screen multiplex cinema. There's a large supermarket and busy Sunday market and plenty of car parking space.

Public Transport: Service 47A operated by Brighton Blue Bus/Local Rider hourly with NO service on Sunday.

The Master Mariner, Brighton Marina.

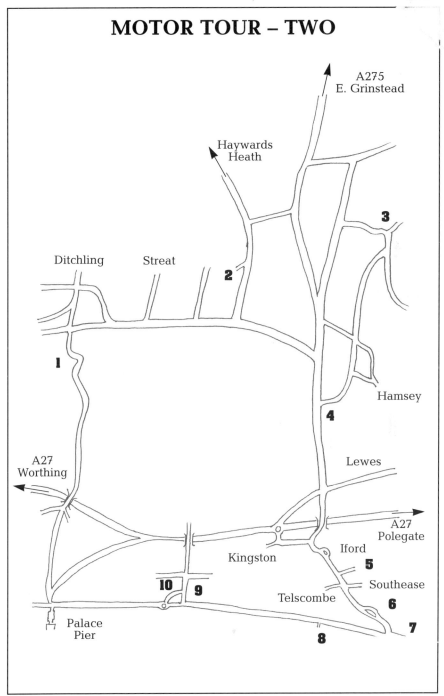

MOTOR TOUR – TWO

A275
E. Grinstead

Haywards
Heath

Ditchling   Streat

2

3

Hamsey

4

A27
Worthing

Lewes

A27
Polegate

Iford

Kingston

5

10   **9**

Southease

6

Telscombe

Palace
Pier

8

7

1

MOTOR TOUR - TWO (51¹/₂ MILES/82.6KM)

BRIGHTON - DITCHLING BEACON - EAST CHILTINGTON
BARCOMBE - OFFHAM - RODMELL - PIDDINGHOE - NEWHAVEN
PEACEHAVEN - ROTTINGDEAN - OVINGDEAN - BRIGHTON

1. Palace Pier - Ditchling Beacon (8¹/₂ miles/13.6km)

Leave Brighton via A27 signposted Lewes. Turn left into St Peters Place immediately after St Peters church then right into Ditchling Road. Keep straight ahead past Hollingbury Castle on the right and at the T-junction turn left then right signposted Ditchling (Beacon). The car park is on the left.

2. Ditchling Beacon - East Chiltington (8 miles/12.9 km)

Descend to the crossroads where turn right along a narrow lane before joining the B2116 at Westmeston, where there is no available parking. In about a mile (1.6km) a road off left leads to Streat. Streat Place and church are about 1¹/₄ miles (2km) along this road where there is limited parking. Retrace route back to the B2116 along which is a magnificent view of the 'V' on the Downs (see page 66). Turn left signposted Plumpton where again there is no available parking, and in 1¹/₂ miles (2.4km) turn left at Novington Lane signposted East Chiltington. In another 1¹/₂ miles (2.4km) turn left signposted thirteenth century church along Chapel Lane where there is parking beside the church.

3. East Chiltington - Barcombe (5¹/₄ miles/8.4km)

Return to Novington Lane and turn left. In 1¹/₂ mile (2.4km) turn right into Honeypot Lane signposted Chailey and at the A275 turn left signposted North Chailey. In little over ¹/₂ mile (0.8km) turn right at Markstakes Lane signposted Barcombe, turning right again in about a mile (1.6km) and left in another 2 miles (3.2km) following all signs for Barcombe. The car park is another mile (1.6km) further on in the village, on the right just past the Royal Oak public house.

4. Barcombe - Offham (4¹/₂ miles/7.2km)

Right out of the car park and right again at the mini roundabout. In ¹/₂ mile (0.8km) turn right signposted Hamsey and in about ³/₄ mile (1.2km) turn left into car park to visit Barcombe church. Continue ahead to T-junction where turn left signposted Offham. Another 1¹/₂ miles (2.4km) to a left turn down Whitefield Lane and through the hamlet of Hamsey. At the T-junction turn left through Hamsey Farm to visit the church (which is kept locked but the key is available from the farm) or right to continue the tour, turning left at the next T-junction following the road to Offham where there is restricted parking on the verge just before the church. Better to turn left at the A275 signposted Lewes and stop at the Chalk Pit Inn a little further along on the right.

5. Offham - Rodmell (7¼ miles/11.7km)

Continue along the A275 to Lewes turning right at the traffic lights in about a mile (1.6km). Keep straight ahead at the roundabout on the A27 signposted Kingston, turning right at The Street in Kingston, past The Juggs public house to visit the church and return. At the next T-junction turn right signposted Newhaven and in ¾ mile (1.2km) turn left signposted Iford where there is limited parking by the church. Continue the loop back to the Newhaven road where turn left and in a mile (1.6km) left again in Rodmell beside the Abergavenney Arms where there is a car park about ½ mile (0.8km) further along on the right.

6. Rodmell - Piddinghoe (3½ miles/5.6km)

Left out of the car park and left again at the T-junction signposted Newhaven. In little over ½ mile (0.8km) turn right signposted Telscombe Village where there is very limited parking by the church (see page 41). Retrace route back to T-junction where turn right then left almost immediately to Southease where there is limited parking round right on the green in front of the church (see page 41). Continue along a road marked "Unsuitable for Motors" turning left at the T-junction for Newhaven. In 1½ mile (2.4km) bear left for Piddinghoe where there is a small car park beside the church.

7. Piddinghoe - Newhaven (2 miles/3.2km)

Continue through the village rejoining the Newhaven road which merges into the A259. Keep to the offside lane where a car park leads off right in a few yards. To visit the fort follow the ring road round right turning left at South Road singposted Newhaven Fort.

8. Newhaven - Peacehaven (2½ miles/4km)

Rejoin the A259 ring road signposted Peacehaven. Turn left at Horsham Avenue to view the Meridian Monument.

9. Peacehaven - Rottingdean (3 miles/4.8km)

Return to the A259 and turn left. In 2 miles (3.2km) Saltdean Lido is passed on the right (parking available if required) and a mile (1.6km) *further on is Rottingdean. A long stay car park is on the left just before the traffic lights and a short stay (3 hours maximum) on the right at the traffic lights.*

10. Rottingdean - Ovingdean (2¹/₄ miles/3.6km)

Continue along the B2123 to Woodingdean turning off left in 1¹/₂ miles (2.4km) to Ovingdean, keeping ahead as the road swings off left to limited parking by the church.

11. Ovingdean - Brighton (4³/₄ miles/7.6km)

Continue to the roundabout on the A259 turning right signposted Brighton. Follow the coast road back to Palace Pier to conclude the tour.

POINTS OF INTEREST DURING THE TOUR

1. Ditchling Beacon

At 227 metres (750 feet) this is the second highest point on the South Downs. It was once an Iron Age hillfort using the steep northern slope as a natural defence and although most of it has been damaged by modern farming and erosion evidence still exists of its whereabouts. As

Looking eastwards from Ditchling Beacon.

its name suggests the Beacon was one of a chain of fires lit to warn of the Spanish Armada. There are extensive views over the Weald from here and on an exceptionally clear day the Hog's Back above Guildford can be seen 31 miles (50km) away.

Public Transport: No public transport serves the Beacon. No toilets or refreshments available other than ice cream.

2. East Chiltington

The village is clustered round its twelfth century church and has not changed much over the last couple of centuries. The surrounding countryside is some of the loveliest in Sussex with a number of historic manors and houses dating back to the Norman Conquest. The Jolly Sportsman freehouse has been converted from a cottage to an alehouse and until recently doubled as the village shop. It was also used as the village hall when the inhabitants sold off their village hall for a housing development and is still used as a polling station whenever there is an election.

Public Transport: No public transport serves the village

Walk: A lovely 6 mile (9.6km) walk through pleasant parkland and across open countryside including Plumpton Agricultural College and the secluded hamlet of Streat (see page 63). Toilets and refreshments at the Jolly Sportsman.

3. Barcombe

The Romans called the village Bercham although Barcombe is really three villages in one. The old community congregated near the church of St Mary the Virgin where Christians have gathered for worship for over a thousand years. When the Black Death ravaged the land many of the population died and those who survived moved away to build new homes for themselves at Barcombe Cross a mile (1.6km) from the original hamlet. The church still survives today as does a Sussex Barn and thatched Round House with the Court House standing behind them. On the far side of the village pond two farmworkers' cottages have been converted into a modern dwelling and two other old cottages on the road to Barcombe Cross still survive.

Barcombe Mills near the derelict railway and the River Ouse is the third community and the flour mill here by the river was mentioned in Domesday Book. The last working mill was built on the site in 1870 and ceased grinding corn in 1934. It became a button factory owned by a

German and run by Italians and became a major source of employment in the villge. With the onset of war the factory was completely destroyed by a mysterious fire in the early hours of Friday March 10th 1939.

Barcombe Place was at one time a Dr Barnado's home for girls and many of them married local men and settled down in the village.

Public Transport: Barcombe Cross is served by Lewes Coaches operating service 22 Lewes - Newick route with buses running two-hourly during the day from Lewes Bus Station except Sunday. There is NO direct service from Brighton to Barcombe Cross.

Walk: A pleasant 7¹/₄ mile (11.7km) walk takes in Barcombe Mills, the River Ouse and popular Anchor Inn with the choice of a shortened version (5³/₄ miles/9.2km) back across a picturesque weir and water meadow.
Toilet and refreshments available in Barcombe Cross.

4. Offham

Pronounced 'Oafham' this sleepy little village lives more in the past than for the future. The busy A275 divides the pretty flint cottages and it is hard to believe that the industrial revolution hit this place in a big way and yet it does go down on record as being the scene of a remarkable piece of engineering and home to one of the first 'railways' in Southern England!

Disused railway tunnels, Chalk pits, Offham.

In the early 1800's George Shiffner of Coombe Place owned the village chalk pit. He was anxious to improve on the horse and cart method of transporting his chalk and lime down the steep hillside to the River Ouse 400 feet (120m) below, so he commissioned William Jessop to solve his problem and in 1809 the Offham tramway was opened.

Operating on a funicular basis, loaded wagons were attached to cables and rolled on rails down a 1 in 2 gradient controlled by a large wheel at the top which simultaneously pulled up an empty wagon on an adjacent track. The wagons ascended and descended through two brick tunnels 7 feet (2.1m) wide which passed under the road below the chalk pit. At the bottom the wagons were put on a turntable, disgorged their wares into a waiting barge and were pulled up empty again. A canal was cut from the Ouse which the barges navigated taking Shiffner's produce to the port at Newhaven.

With the coming of the conventional railway system waterway traffic diminished and the Offham tramway closed down in 1870. Traces of its existence are still evident today with good views of the tunnel entrances in the car park of the Chalk Pit public house where toilets and refreshments are available.

Public Transport: Service 21 and 22 Lewes - Newick operated by Lewes Coaches run hourly during the day except Sunday. There is NO direct service from Brighton to Offham.

The Juggs Arms, Kingston.

5. Rodmell

How this delightful little village got is name is speculative. Legend has it the Mill was the source of its name but there is no mill here today just the memory of its existence in the name Mill Road. Gone too is Rodmell Place, home of the de la Chambre family in the sixteenth and seventeenth centuries, but a brass in their memory still exists in the twelfth century church. Still to be seen too is the old smithy on the crossroads whose present incumbent has atttained some recognition for his shepherd's crooks.

Monk's House, Rodmell.

Perhaps the most renowned building in the village is Monk's House, bought in 1919 by Leonard and Virginia Woolf, leading lights of the literary Bloomsbury group. Many literary greats of the day visited this humble country retreat - oil lamps provided light and a well was the only source of water - including T.S. Eliot.

The Woolfs spent their time between here and London until 1940 when their town residence was bombed. The following year Virginia drowned herself in the Ouse and her ashes are buried in the garden of Monk's House. Leonard remained here until his death in 1969 and the House is now the property of the National Trust and open to the public.

Hours of Opening: Wednesdays and Saturdays, 2-5pm April and October, 2-6pm May-September. Admission charge. Telephone: 01273 472385.

Public Transport: Service 123 Lewes - Newhaven - Peacehaven operated by the County Rider connects with Brighton and Hove/Stagecoach services 711 and 712 Brighton - Eastbourne - Folkestone except Sundays at Newhaven and Peacehaven but it is advisable to confirm exact times before travelling.

Walk: A 7¹/₄ mile (11.7km) jaunt along the South Downs Way to Kingston and back along the Ouse valley through Swanborough and Iford begins from the car park just beyond Monk's House (see page 71).
Toilets and refreshments available at the Abergavenny Arms.

Telscombe

A perfect piece of England this! unspoiled and in complete contrast to the urban development going on all around. There is no through road and despite numerous campaigns to provide one the narrow lane used to approach the village simply peters out at a spot famous for its bank of wild daffodils in springtime.

Ambrose Gorham is the man responsible for this idyllic situation. A retired bookmaker he became squire and benefactor of Telscombe at the end of the nineteenth century. He refused any development while improving the condition and facilities of the village, laying in mains water in 1909 and electricity in 1930. Telscombe was the first village in East Sussex to have electricity and its church the first to be floodlit.

He never lost his love of racing, training many winners at his Telscombe stables and his most famous product was 'Shannon Lass' which won the Grand National in 1902.

When he died in 1933 Gorham bequeathed all his land to Brighton Corporation on trust, stating in his will that the purpose of the gift was to preserve the rural nature of the village. The trust exists to this day ensuring Telscombe retains its tranquility and individuality.

Southease

The simple church, another of the three referred to at Piddinghoe with its Norman round tower, looks down on the village green which lacks something in its presentation to make it the envy of Sussex. Perhaps it retains its appearance from the far off days when a little girl who was to become the most famous Englishwoman ever used to run and play here, for Elizabeth I spent some of her childhood hereabouts. The church goes some way to compensate however with its Norman influence,

Piddinghoe Church with its rare circular tower.

Tudor Window and Jacobean carving. Scant remains of the original thriteenth century wall decoration show that they must have been elaborate and beautiful in their day.

6. Piddinghoe

An old smuggling haunt this, set beside the Ouse and only three miles (4.8km) from the sea it had an ideal location to prosper from contraband.

A more down to earth source of employment however were the brickworks (pardon the pun), now long since disappeared, although in the grounds of Kiln Cottage on the northern outskirts of the village is the only remaining bottle-shaped kiln in the county.

The church is one of only three in Sussex with a round tower built of flint and all of them stand in the Ouse valley (the others are at Southease and St Michael's in Lewes). The weather vane was immortalised by Rudyard Kipling in his poem "Sussex" with the line 'Where windy Piddinghoe's begilded dolphin veers'. The fact that he got it wrong doesn't seem to matter for as any local will tell you it is not a dolphin but a salmon trout.

Public Transport: The same service serves Piddinghoe and Southease as Rodmell. Telscombe is not served by any public transport.
No toilets or refreshments available.

7. Newhaven

Iron Age dwellers built a fort here on Castle Hill overlooking the present harbour mouth but it wasn't so strategically placed then as the present Fort is today. Four hundred years ago the Sussex Ouse ended a thirty mile flow from its Wealden tributatries at Seaford. A storm in 1579 blocked the mouth of the river with shingle isolating the port and forcing it to burst its way through a new outlet to the sea. The new outlet was near to Meeching, a village established by the Saxons on the river bank below the Iron Age hillfort, and the new harbour became known as New Haven and with it began the foundation for the present town's future prosperity.

In the early years oak from the great local Wealden forests were the chief exports and slab ice a major import. Two ice-houses existed in the town and the cargo was hoisted into wagons which were hauled by donkeys along a metal track long before the first railway was laid in 1847. Shipbuilding and breweries were the town's main industries until the coming of the nineteenth century saw its importance as a cross-channel seaport. With the advent of the rail link to London a service to Dieppe was soon started with paddle steamers taking as long as seven hours to complete the crossing. Once more modern turbine driven ships were introduced the crossing time was cut to under three hours and the port continued to prosper.

The Fort was commissioned by Lord Palmerston in the 1860's to counter any hostile threat from the French but none ever materialised.

Newhaven Harbour and Marina.

Built into the chalk hillside it features gun emplacements, mortar batteries, magazines and a labyrinth of underground passages. It renewed its defensive role during both World Wars and was decommissioned in 1962, after which it fell into disrepair. In 1979 it was classed an ancient monument and restoration work began two years later. Today it houses a military museum, children's assault course and boasts magnificent views along the channel.

The twelfth century church of St Michael with its heavily beamed roof and supporting timber columns along with the adjacent Old Rectory and surrounding brick and flint walls are all listed buildings within this conservation area of the town. In the churchyard some curious sculptured gravestones catch the eye including one, an obelisk capped with fishes, shells and seaweed to the crew of the war-sloop *Brazen* which went down off Newhaven in 1799 with 106 men on board and all bar one were lost.

The Bridge Inn began life as the New Inn when it was built in 1623 and so remained for 150 years until a drawbridge was built to replace the ferry crossing of the Ouse. In premises now part of the exisiting building Thomas Tipper brewed his famous ales which he regularly supplied to George IV at the Royal Pavilion in Brighton. Tipper contributed quite generously to the construction costs of the drawbridge and when he died in 1785 they carved a replica of it on his tombstone which can still be seen in the churchyard of St Michael.

Royal visitors to the Inn in 1848 signed the register as Mr and Mrs Smith. They were in fact Louis Phillipe and Marie Amelie deposed King and Queen of France who were shipped into Newhaven after fleeing mob rule back home.

A small **Local and Maritime Museum** formerly on the west foreshore and now situated in a new building at Garden Paradise, Avis Way displays photographs and items of local interest relating to the port, shipwrecks and wartime role and general history of the town. It is operated by the Newhaven Historical Society and is packed with items of nostalgia and interest.

Hours of Opening: **Newhaven Fort** *open Easter-October, Wednesday-Sunday and Bank Holidays, 10.30am-6pm (Daily during school holidays), Toilets and picnic facilities available. Telephone: 01273 517622.*

Hours of Opening: **Local and Maritime Museum** *open from 10.30am-5pm, Wednesday, Saturday, Sunday and Bank Holidays, all year round. Telephone: 01273 612530*

Public Transport: Service 712 Brighton-Eastbourne (and 711 to Folkestone) operated by Brighton and Hove Buses/Stagecoach every half hour during the day Monday-Saturday and every hour in the evenings and on Sunday.

8. Peacehaven

Founded by Charles William Neville when, before the Great War, he bought some 600 acres of land from the Marquis of Abergavenny which he divided into building plots and accompanying roads. Then, founding the South Coast Land and Resort Company, Neville offered the land to the public through the national press in the form of a competition in order to find a name for this new "Garden City by the Sea". The winning name was New Anzac on Sea influenced by the fact that a detachment of the Australian and New Zealand Army Corps were based here during the War. The tragic events at Gallipoli gave cause for feelings of misgivings and it was decided to drop New Anzac as a name for the area and hold a second competition instead: Peacehaven was the second successful entry.

Today it is a conglomeration of flats, bungalows and houses accommodating much of Brighton's overspill. Neville's dream never really materialised and Peacehaven grew in size beyond anyone's expectation.

The Meridian Monument situated on the Promenade at the end of Horsham Avenue is the only real point of interest in the area, the present monument being built in 1936 to replace an earlier wooden erection standing

Meridian Monument, Peacehaven.

astride the line of the Prime Meridian of Greenwich - the international date line - where it leaves the coast.

Toilets and refreshments available.

Public Transport: Service 712 Brighton-Eastbourne operated by Brighton and Hove Buses/Stagecoach every half hour during the day, hourly in the evenings and on Sunday.

9. Rottingdean

There has been a settlement at Rottingdean (The Valley of Rota's people) since early Saxon times. It was given to William de Warrene, Lord of Lewes, for his support of the Conqueror at the Battle of Hastings and has been the home of many famous characters in more recent times.

Rudyard Kipling lived at The Elms between 1897-1903 and wrote some of his best works here until incessant sightseers got on his nerves and he "escaped" to Batemans where he lived the rest of his life. His aunt lived at Prospect House (now North End House); she was Lady Burne-Jones, wife of the painter Sir Edward Burne-Jones leader of the Pre-Raphaelites. Sir Roderick Jones was another resident at North End House. He became chairman of Reuter's the worldwide News Agency started by a German bank clerk before the days of telegrams and electricity who also made Rottingdean his home. Enid Bagnold, novelist and playwright, was Sir Roderick's wife and achieved fame with "The Chalk Garden" and "National Velvet".

The Grange, now the library and museum, was once the home of Sir William Nicholson painter and friend of Kipling. Later alterations to the house were designed by Sir Edwin Lutyens, consultant architect to the then owner Sir George Lewis.

Challoners is the oldest house in the village for records show that in 1456 it was a manor house. Tallboys was once the Custom House and the village was once the centre for smugglers and their contraband. They often met at the Black Horse and White Horse Inns to plan their operations and Dr Hooker, much respected vicar of the parish, would often act as look-out on his fast grey mare whenever there was a run-in at the Gap.

The present White Horse Inn was built in 1934 when the original 16th century coaching inn was demolished. In those days it offered stabling for forty horses and was often used as auction rooms with cargo and remains of shipwrecks being sold here.

The village green and pond have also existed for several centuries and at one time farmers brought their flocks of sheep down from the hills to drink from the pond.

Opposite St Margarets Church dates from 1080. Legend has it marauding French pirates raided what is now the High Street in 1377 sending many of the villagers to seek refuge in the church tower. The pirates set fire to the tower and those inside perished and the reddish tinge seen on the stonework today is said to have been caused by the extreme heat of their barbaric act. Almost five hundred years later Stanley Baldwin was married in the church in 1892. He became Prime Minister in the 1930's and returned to Rottingdean on his golden

Rottingdean Village.

jubilee to present a commemorative chair to the church which still stands in the chancel.

Whippng Post Lane beside the Plough Inn now has a horse chestnut tree to mark the spot where the village whipping post once stood.

There are ample places of refreshment in the village along with adequate toilet facilities.

Walk: A fascinating walk begins from the village passing the old smock mill, Roedean School, Ovingdean and visiting the lost village of Balsdean. The walk covers a figure of eight circuit so may be split into two separate walks if desired.

Public Transport: Service 712 Brighton-Eastbourne operated by Brighton and Hove Buses/Stagecoach every half hour during the day and hourly in the evenings and on Sunday.

10. Ovingdean

Mentioned in Domesday Book as a dwelling for 14 souls Ovingdean (the valley of Ofa's people) is believed to have been one of the earliest Saxon settlements in the area. Even today it is still classed a hamlet and has never had a public house.

The earliest buildings were all grouped round the church which was built between 1066-1086 and made entirely of flint and shingle, a unique combination in Sussex. Much of the present day paintwork and stained glass in the church of St Wulfran is by Charles Kempe whose coat of arms hangs in the nave and whose shield of three wheat sheaves acts as a signature to his work. Kempe also designed and made the family tomb in the churchyard in which he is now interred.

Buried nearby is Magnus Volk inventor of Britains first electric railway from Brighton's Palace Pier to Black Rock (see page 7).

Of the buildings grouped round the church Ovingdean Grange Farm was the oldest with parts dating back to the sixteenth century still standing. Harrison Ainsworth wrote a novel called "Ovingdean Grange" in which Charles II is supposed to have taken refuge prior to fleeing abroad although there is nothing in history to support the author's views.

Ovingdean Hall was built in 1786 by Kempe's father Nathaniel who was the uncle of Thomas Read Kempe who built Kemp Town in Brighton. It was 1914 before any other buildings were erected anywhere in the area.

The Grange, Rottingdean.

WALK 1 – DEVIL'S DYKE

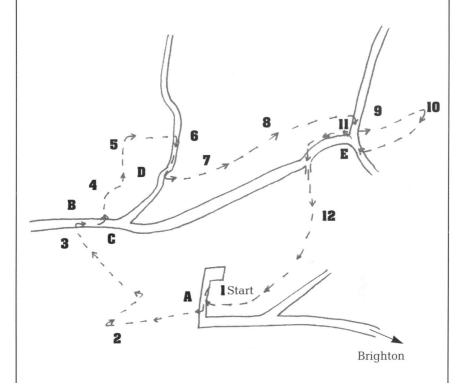

A South Downs Way
B Spring
C Fulking
D South Downs
E Poynings Church

WALK 1 – DEVIL'S DYKE

Parking:	Ample parking at the Dyke Hotel
Map Reference:	Landranger 198 grid reference 258111
Distance:	5¹/₂ miles (8.8km)
Time to Allow:	2¹/₂ hours
Terrain:	Along well used tracks across the South Downs and well defined paths elsewhere with a steep descent into Fulking and steep ascent back along the Dyke.
Toilets/Refreshments:	Dyke Hotel; Shepherd and Dog public house, Fulking or Royal Oak public house, Poynings.
Route:	Devil's Dyke – South Downs Way – Fulking – Poynings – Devil's Dyke

A short stretch along the South Downs Way starts this walk with breathtaking views across the Weald from one of the most dramatic escarpments along the entire length of the Downs. A steep descent along a narrow hollow in the face of the Downs ends at the Shepherd and Dog public house, Fulking alongside which is the fascinating spring that never fails to gush water even in the most catastrophic droughts. The route continues across open fields towards the wooded summit of Newtimber Hill before turning sharply towards the next village of Poynings with its 14th Century church that has remained largely unaltered throughout its life. The final ascent along the length of the Dyke provides a fitting conclusion to this splendid outing.

Directions:

1. *Walk back along the road past the head of Devil's Dyke on the left to where the South Downs Way* **(A)** *crosses and turn right across the field where the ramparts of the old hill fort are on the right with triangulation point atop of them. Bear left to a gate in the corner of the field and continue for about ¹/₂ mile (0.8km) to a point where an obvious track merges in from the left opposite a raised mound which is an old Iron Age Tumulus.*
2. *At the public footpath signpost immediately beyond the tumulus turn sharp right downhill on a sunken track between high banks and at a signposted cross-tracks about half way down the side of the hill turn sharp left keeping alongside the fence on the right. Pass through a belt of scrubland then over a stile before bearing left into the Shepherd and Dog public house car park where the spring* **(B)** *is to the left.*

3. *Turn right past the pub into Fulking* **(C)** *turning left immediately after The Fountain through a gate and across the grassy recreational area to a stile in the wooden railings, bearing diagonally right across the next field (or round the right hand edge if easier).*

4. *Pass through a gap in the right hand corner of the field and over a culvert keeping along the right hand edge of the next field. Cross the stile in the corner and turn left following the left hand edge of a field with the South Downs* **(D)** *behind you.*

5. *Cross four more stiles before entering a paddock keeping ahead in the direction of the public footpath signpost as the hedge veers away to the left. Remain ahead crossing a stile and a plank bridge over a stream immediately beyond which turn right alongside the stream before finally passing through an overgrown area to road.*

6. *Turn right here and in about 250 yards (230m) turn left over a stile beside a metal field gate.*

7. *Keep slightly left uphill to a stile in the left hand corner of the field keeping ahead across the next field towards the wooded summit of Newtimber Hill.*

8. *Cross another stile before bearing left to a bridge across a stream. Keep alongside the hedge on the left then along a track by the sewerage plant to road.*

9. *Turn right at the road and in 60 yards (55m) go left on a metalled track through a school playground, passing to the left of the school hall. Pass over a stile before continuing along the left edge of the next field. In the next field corner cross a stile and a stream then head across the next field towards a cottage nestling at the foot of Newtimber Hill.*

10. *Turn sharp right immediately before reaching the gate following the left hand edge of the field and aiming for the farm buildings ahead a little to the left of Poynings church. At the farm veer right of the Dutch barn passing through the farmyard and out to the road opposite Poynings Church* **(E)***.*

11. *Pass through the stone archway across the road and turn left along a footpath to the Royal Oak public house, Poynings. About 50 yards (45m) beyond the pub turn left almost opposite the entrance to Dyke Farm House along a metalled lane which soon becomes a rough track.*

12. *At the foot of the steep wooded slope of the Downs take the left hand track of three following it up through woodland to the scrub covered hillside along the edge of Devil's Dyke back to the road where turn right back to the car park.*

Devil's Dyke.

POINTS OF INTEREST ON THE WALK

(A) South Downs Way

This was one of six long distance footpaths recommended by a special committee on Footpaths and Access to the Countryside in 1947 with an original intention that the route should stretch from Eastbourne – at the start of the South Downs – to Winchester where it would join the Pilgrims Way, and continue to a point west of Salisbury. Fifteen years later the National Parks Commission (the predecessor to the Countryside Commission) submitted a proposal to the Minister of Housing and Local Government for the route to stretch from Eastbourne to the West Sussex county boundary near Buriton and that was duly approved the following year.

On 15th July 1972 the South Downs Way was officially opened by Lord Shawcross albeit with an alternative route, the footpath following the cliffs over Beachy Head and the Seven Sisters to Cuckmere Haven and from there over the hills to join the original route near Alfriston.

The Way is by no means a new route for the greater part of it was already in existence even when the special committee deliberated back in 1947, for much of it is ancient trackway that has now been made accessible to man and horse along its entirety.

Waymarkers of various kinds direct the user, in some instances merely by the use of an acorn sign, the Commission's long distance route symbol.

(B) Spring (Fulking)

The spring gushes out of the steep hillside in a copse just above the Shepherd and Dog public house and in the old days of sheep-rearing the stream used to be dammed in the hollow and a sheepwash made in the bend in the lane. When operations came to an end for the day the men involved would walk to the pub stiff with cold and wringing wet which is why it is so named. On the side of the wellhouse in Victorian tiles is the text 'He sendeth springs into the valleys which run among the hills. Oh that men would praise the Lord for His goodness'. Unfortunately the tile setter put three of the "S's" upside down, but it does make it look all the more rustic in doing so.

(C) Fulking

A pretty little village with paint-washed cottages and thatch aplenty yet unusually without a church. At the beginning of the 19th Century sheep outnumbered humans ten to one in the area and as if that wasn't enough sheep many other downland villages sent their sheep to be washed in the spring dip during May and June prior to the annual shearing.

(D) South Downs

The creation of the Downs began many millions of years ago with volcanoes and earth movements forming a platform of Palaeozoic rocks. Through time this platform acted as the foundation for a series of sedimentary deposits from the water of a great freshwater lake which through pressure, were consolidated into rock strata. Then the land slowly sank allowing the sea to flood the area and a chalky sediment appeared, much of it from the shells of minute sea creatures called Foraminifera which sank to the bottom as they ended their short lives, their soft bodies dissolving leaving the detritus of their shells to add to the build up of chalk. This was known as the Cretaceous period which lasted a very long time for the beds of chalk it created were hundreds of metres thick.

The Eocene period followed when the deposits were of sand and clay which covered the chalk also to a considerable depth.

Vast earth movements brought this peaceful deposition period to an abrupt end, resulting in the Alps in central Europe and creating a huge dome stretching from France to Hampshire and back as far as the North Downs in Kent. With the sedimentary strata now exposed to erosion from the wind and rain our present Downs landscapes developed.

(E) Poynings

The 14th Century church of the Holy Trinity was built under the will of Michael de Poynygges, Lord of the Manor, who died in 1369 and from whom the village takes its name. There are medieval tiles in the altar steps and there are a few battered old beams, one dated 1625, while the font is 15th century with Gothic ornaments and Jacobean cover but the real gem is a tiny carved oak almsbox made in 1760 and brought from a convent on the continent.

George Beard was probably rector for the longest period here, 54 years in the 18th Century, although it is said he used only two texts for his sermons throughout his entire incumbency. Those who succeeded him found a very neglected church and from the beginning of the 19th Century much restoration work was carried out.

Wolstonbury Hill.

WALK 2 – WOLSTONBURY HILL

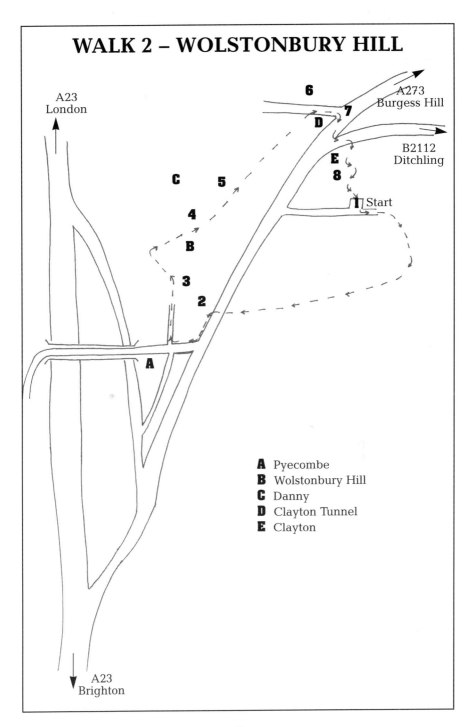

A Pyecombe
B Wolstonbury Hill
C Danny
D Clayton Tunnel
E Clayton

WALK 2 – WOLSTONBURY HILL

Parking:	Car park beside Jack and Jill Windmills, Clayton
Map Reference:	Landranger 198 grid reference 302135
Distance:	6 miles (9.6km)
Time to Allow:	2½ hours
Terrain:	Along well used tracks on the South Downs Way with a steady ascent up Wolstonbury Hill and fairly steep descent the other side. The stretch of track to Clayton could be muddy in wet weather and the final part of the route is quite a climb back to the car park.
Toilets/Refreshments:	Plough Inn, Pyecombe
Route:	Clayton Windmills – South Downs Way – Pyecombe – Wolstonbury Hill – Clayton Tunnel – Clayton – Clayton Windmills

Beginning with an easy stretch of the South Downs Way on its gradual descent into Pyecombe the walk then begins a steady climb up the slopes of Wolstonbury Hill to the Iron Age hillfort at its summit. The views from here are magnificent with the twin windmills away to the east and the whole of the Weald before us. A fairly steep path leads the way down across the fields to the bridleway which emerges at the main road by the fascinating entrance to Clayton railway tunnel. The final part of the walk passes through the tiny hamlet of Clayton back to the windmills above.

Directions:

1. *Turn left out of the car park then right at the fork onto the South Downs Way, turning right at the cross-tracks and following the Way down to the main road.*

2. *Cross the road and turn left at the South Downs Way signpost following the path right into Pyecombe* **(A)**. *Turn right at the crossroads up The Wyshe to the National Trust sign at Wolstonbury Hill* **(B)**.

3. *Turn left at the cross-tracks by the NT sign then right at the next public footpath signpost to the summit of Wolstonbury Hill. The large house seen to the left is Danny* **(C)**.

4. *Leave the summit in the direction of the windmills crossing the stile to the left of the metal gate, keeping ahead at the cross-tracks then*

*through the squeeze stile and continuing ahead alongside the fence
on the right.*

5. *Over another stile and up to the public bridleway where turn left
then left again through a gate (this stretch may be muddy after wet
weather).*

6. *Turn right at the metalled lane to the main road where the Clayton
Tunnel* **(D)** *is down right.*

7. *Turn right at the main road then left at the junction to Lewes before
turning right across the playing field to the church of St John the
Baptist, Clayton* **(E).**

8. *Turn right out of the church then right again at the public bridleway
sign back to the Windmills and car park.*

POINTS OF INTEREST ON THE WALK

(A) Pyecombe (see page 24)

(B) Wolstonbury Hill

At 670 feet (205m) Wolstonbury Hill stands clear of the line of the South
Downs and is a landmark for miles around. Its summit is encircled by
the ramparts of an Iron Age hillfort the views from which are superb
with the Ashdown Forest and the Weald to the north-east and the
Surrey Hills to the north-west.

(C) Danny

The original manorhouse was probably not on the site of the existing
Elizabethan mansion begun in 1582 by Sir Thomas Goring and finished
in 1595 but well have been where its stables are now.

Built of mellow red Tudor brick with stone dressings, mullioned
windows and gabled roofs the north wing encloses an earlier house four
storeys high, containing the original staircase, some ornamental plaster
ceilings and Elizabethan ribbed barrel vaulting.

In the Civil War the Gorings, staunch Royalists, lost everything. Their
estate was forfeit to the Commonwealth whose land speculators sold
Danny, its outbuildings and 160 acres of land to the Courthorpes of Kent
for £550. The Courthorpes lived at Danny until the death of Peter
Courthorpe in 1724 when the property passed to his heiress, Barbara.

Henry Campion married Barbara and the South front (facing
Wolstonbury Hill) was much altered by them. In 1728 the entire side
was given a Queen Anne facing with three ranges of windows,
completely different from the East front. The screens and panelling in

the Great Hall, staircase in the South wing and additions to the West side of the mansion were installed at the same time. Successive generations of the Campions played the role of squire for 200 years until the Great War of 1914-18.

In 1918 the War Cabinet met here presided over by Lloyd George and the Armistice Terms were drawn up at the large oak table in the Great Hall.

During the Second World War the house was occupied by British and Canadian troops and from 1947, within the same family ownership, Danny was let as a school for seven or eight years. In the 1960s it provided accommodation for retired and semi-retired professional people.

Hours of Opening: The Great Hall, public rooms and the gardens, Wednesday and Thursdays between 1400-1700 (May-September). Access is between Hassocks and Hurstpierpoint on the B2116 off New Way Lane. Telephone: 01273 833000.

(D) Clayton Tunnel

The tunnel cost £90,000 to build and is $1^1/_4$ miles (2.1km) long. Apart from its castellated portals with arrowslits and battlemented turrets guarding its entrance (the cottage between the turrets is a later addition and was, until recently, occupied) the tunnel is best known for a terrible accident which happened on Sunday 25th August 1861. Three trains were involved in the pile up which was blamed on errors made by overworked signalmen and twenty three passengers died in the carnage.

(E) Clayton

Nestling at the foot of the Downs the quaint little church of St John the Baptist was begun by Saxons and still has one of only two perfect Saxon arches in Sussex. Above it are some of the earliest wall paintings in Britain, running along three walls of the nave and some of the figures are clear and well preserved dating from the 13th Century. Norman Hartnell, dress designer to Her Majesty the Queen for many years, is buried in the humble little churchyard.

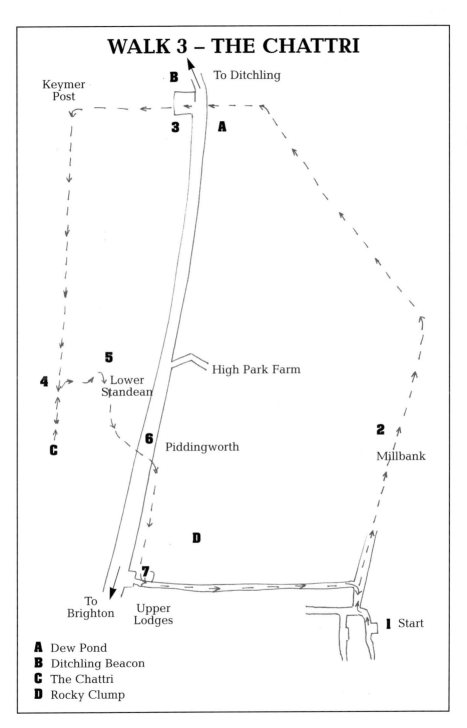

WALK 3 – THE CHATTRI

B

To Ditchling

Keymer Post

3

A

5

4

Lower Standean

High Park Farm

C

2

Millbank

6

Piddingworth

D

Rocky Clump

7

To Brighton

Upper Lodges

I Start

A Dew Pond
B Ditchling Beacon
C The Chattri
D Rocky Clump

WALK 3 – THE CHATTRI

Parking:	Stanmer Park (where there is unlimited parking)
Map Reference:	Landranger 198 grid reference 337097
Distance:	8½ miles (14km)
Time to Allow:	4 hours
Terrain:	A steady ascent to Ditchling Beacon along well defined paths across open donwland then across undulating countryside to the Chattri and back to Stanmer Park along a quiet country lane.
Toilets/Refreshments:	Stanmer village
Route:	Stanmer village - Millbank - Ditchling Beacon - Keymer Post - The Chattri - Lower Standean - Piddingworth - Upper Lodges - Stanmer village.

Beginning through the village street flanked with flint cottages and a working farm the route soon begins the gradual ascent of the Downs to the majestic Ditchling Beacon where the South Downs Way takes us west to Keymer Post the official boundary between East and West Sussex. A path heading towards the coast gives access to the Chattri before returning through Lower Standean to the Upper Lodges on the edge of Stanmer Park and then back to Stanmer village to conclude the walk.

Directions:

1. *Through the village keeping alongside the fence on the right to Millbank.*
2. *Keep ahead signposted Ditchling Beacon, turning left through the second gate to meet the South Downs Way where keep left past the Dew Pond* **(A)** *to Ditchling Beacon* **(B)**
3. *Continue along the South Downs Way to Keymer Post and in 70 yards (63m) turn left at the signpost keeping ahead as far as the field gate.*
4. *Ahead through the gate for ½ mile (0.8km) to visit The Chattri* **(C)** *and return, turning right following the fence on the right before turning right through the gate to Lower Standean.*
5. *Follow the track through the farm before turning left at the signpost. Bear right round the long barn following the track round to the road.*

6. *Cross road and over stile turning right, keeping alongside fence on the left. Cross two more stiles into the woods before reaching the metalled road at Upper Lodges.*
7. *Turn left at road following it past Rocky Clump* **(D)** *on the left back to Stanmer Village where turn right back to car park.*

The Chattri Monument.

POINTS OF INTEREST ON THE WALK

(A) Dew Pond

A dewpond is an artificial clay pond which holds rain water and used by shepherds and farmers to water their stock. They were often built in chalk and limestone areas and the oldest of them date back to the seventeenth century although they were still being made as late as the 1940s. Their builders often worked at night digging the symmetrical hollows before lining them with puddled clay. Good ones retain their water even in the driest of weather for the true art was in the positioning of the pond to collect the maximum amount of rainwater running off the land while allowing for as little evaporation as possible. Contrary to their name they are not designed to gather dew; they are named after their inventor a Mr Dew.

(B) Ditchling Beacon (see page 36)

(C) The Chattri

It was to this desolate spot in the years of the Great War they brought the Hindus and Sikhs who gave their lives fighting for us, setting them on a funeral pyre. The fires were lit on two great stones which are still visible and the white temple of Sicilian marble, its canopy raised on eight ornamental pillars, was built in memory of all the Indians who died in the conflict. Their ashes are on the site of the funeral pyre where they passed through the fire and the temple stands a shining white memory among the green green amphitheatre of the Downs of those who came from the other side of the world and died in a quarrel that was not theirs.

(D) Rock Clump

The small tree plantation has revealed through archaeological excavations to have been used as a settlement around the third century and with the discovery of at least seven graves evidence also shows it to have been used as a burial ground a few centuries later.

WALK 4 – EAST CHILTINGTON

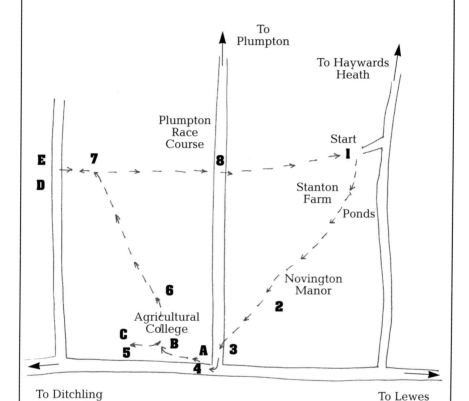

A Half Moon P.H. Plumpton
B Plumpton Place
C Plumpton Church
D Streat
E Streat Place

WALK 4 – EAST CHILTINGTON

Parking:	Minimal parking by the church
Map Reference:	Landranger 198 grid reference 369152
Distance:	6 miles (10km)
Time to Allow:	3 hours
Terrain:	Along tracks and across meadows on fairly level Wealdland
Toilets/Refreshments:	Half Moon public house, Plumpton
Route:	East Chiltington - Stantons Farm - Novington Manor - Half Moon Public House, Plumpton - Plumpton Place - Plumpton Agricultural College - Streat - East Chiltington

Along a private road leading from the church we pass through delightful parkland belonging to Stantons which was built by the Chaloner family in 1570 and is now a farm. Refreshments may be taken en route at the Half Moon public house where an unusual work of art greets the visitor before skirting the impressive Plumpton Place on the edge of Plumpton Agricultural College. An attractive stretch passes through woodland before reaching Streat with its thirteenth century church and Elizabethan manor then the final leg passes Plumpton racecourse back to East Chiltington.

Directions:

1. *From the church keep ahead along a private road to Stanton Farm and Novington Manor which is used as a footpath to Plumpton Lane. Take the right fork by the ponds passing Novington Manor and keeping ahead over the stiles by Stable Cottage.*
2. *Cross the meadow to two more stiles in the right hand corner, over the next field diagonally right before passing through a single hinged lift-up gate then keeping to the hedge on the right and over the stile to the road.*
3. *Turn left at the road and right at the T-junction where the Half Moon Public House* **(A)** *offers refreshments.*
4. *Continue along the public footpath to Plumpton Place* **(B)** *following the yellow waymarkers, turning right to Plumpton Agricultural College where a grassy bank off left leads to the spired church (which is generally kept locked)* **(C)**.
5. *Double back from the church turning left past the students car park.*

6. *Immediately before the track begins to rise ahead turn off left over a stile, continuing diagonally left over a meadow and through a metal gate in the direction of the yellow waymarkers. Over another stile into the woods following the yellow waymarkers along an obvious route.*

7. *Turn left onto the gravel track to Streat* **(D)** *and Streat Place* **(E)** *returning along the same track past the edge of Plumpton Racecourse.*

8. *Cross the road and continue ahead through the woods back to the church at East Chiltington.*

POINTS OF INTEREST ON THE WALK

(A) Half Moon Public House, Plumpton

Built in 1841 this country pub served as a coaching stop on the Ditchling to Offham turnpike until the turn of the nineteenth century. Hanging in the bar over the fireplace is a unique painting of over 100 of the regular patrons which was commissioned in 1978 and painted by Dick Leech of Slaugham.

(B) Plumpton Place

A half-timbered Tudor house the Place is a most impressive building surrounded by a moat, now dry, which had been reduced in stature to being a mere farmhouse at the turn of this century but was thankfully rescued and transformed by Sir Edwin Lutyens. Its most illustrious occupant was Sir Leonard Mascall who during the reign of Henry VIII is said to have introduced golden carp and golden pippins to England here. He wrote many books long before Shakespeare got into print and was a most popular author of his day.

(C) Plumpton Church

Mainly thirteenth century the church is a simple place with nave and chancel, giant buttresses, a low massive tower and a shingled spire. The doorway in the south wall is Norman as is the great square font and there are pale traces of medieval wall paintings which may well have been the work of the monks of Lewes Priory.

(D) Streat

The church is thirteenth century with fourteenth century windows one of which has the shields of the Dobells who lived here showing does and bells. In the floor are iron gravestones made when the foundries of Sussex were consuming all the forest to make iron. The bell is sixteenth century and there are eighteenth century monuments to the owners of Streat Place.

(E) Streat Place

An Elizabethan mansion built on the same site of a much earlier house dating back to before the Conquest and entered in Domesday Book when the hamlet was called Estrat. Walter Dobell gave the house its knapped flint facade in the classic E plan as a gesture to Elizabeth I and the house stayed in the Dobell family until the middle of the eighteenth century during which time it is said to have had a curious hiding place so large that during the Civil War a fugitive Royalist rode into it on horseback and escaped the Roundheads.

The "V" plantation, Streat. The trees were planted to celebrate Queen Victoria's Golden Jubilee in 1887.

WALK 5 – BARCOMBE MILLS

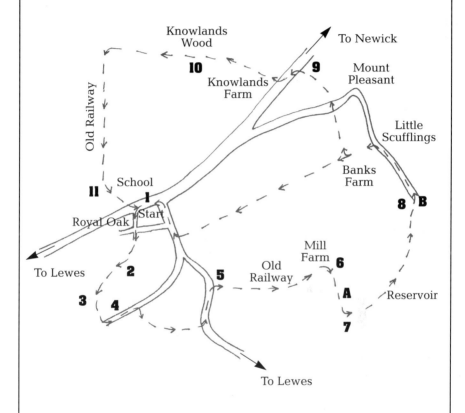

Knowlands Wood

To Newick

10

9

Mount Pleasant

Knowlands Farm

Old Railway

Little Scufflings

Banks Farm

School

11

1

Royal Oak

Start

8 **B**

To Lewes

2

Mill Farm

6

Old Railway

5

A

3

4

Reservoir

7

To Lewes

A Barcombe Mills
B Anchor Inn

WALK 5 – BARCOMBE MILLS

Parking:	Car park just beyond the Royal Oak public house
Map Reference:	Landranger 198 grid reference 421158
Distance:	7¼ miles (11.8km) or 5¾ miles (9.4km)
Time to Allow:	4 hours or 3 hours
Terrain:	Fairly level ground along disused railway track, riverbank, metalled road, meadows and woodland.
Toilets/Refreshments:	Anchor Inn en route or Royal Oak public house, Barcombe Cross
Route:	Barcombe Cross – Barcombe Mills – Anchor Inn – Bank's Farm – (Barcombe Cross) – Mount Pleasant – Knowlands Farm – Knowlands Wood – Disused Railway – Barcombe Cross

The River Ouse plays a significant part in this choice of routes as does the dismantled railway from Lewes to East Grinstead. The decision on whether to complete the full walk or opt for the shortened version is immaterial to the fulfilment of its attraction for indeed the content is so appealing it may well result in the necessity to complete both versions so as not to miss anything.

Beginning with a pleasant stroll to the river, streams and weir at Barcombe Mills the walk then continues along the river bank almost as far at the Anchor Inn returning along the service road to Banks Farm where the choice of routes then has to be made. The shortened version passes through delightful water meadows while the full walk takes in the attractive Knowlands Farm with its adjacent woods and stretch of disused railway.

Directions:

1. *Turn left out of the car park and left again immediately before the Royal Oak public house. Cross straight over at the crossroads taking the public footpath between the backs of houses following the yellow waymarkers along a well defined path along the right edge of a cultivated field.*

2. *Look out for the stile as the high bushes break and turn right over here, turning left almost at once along an obvious path that is unofficial but well used along the old railway. Follow this path down right through a kissing gate and along a path through the woods turning left at the field.*

3. Over stile into the next field which cross to the right of a twin gabled house and along a defined path to the left of a huge oak. Cross another stile, turning left onto a metalled road.

4. Over the old railway bridge and as the road begins to climb look out for a public footpath signpost to the right. Keep alongside the fence on the right across the next field to a stile in the far corner. Keep ahead across the next field to the road, crossing the stile and turning left up the hill.

5. In 150 yards (140m) as the road swings off left turn right through five barred gate, crossing the old railway and across next field before crossing a stile and turning left in the direction of the yellow waymarkers.

6. Turn right by the barns of Mill Farm continuing ahead and approaching Barcombe Mills **(A)** by Pikes Bridge.

7. Turn left through a squeeze gate with the Ouse on the left continuing along the towpath and over a footbridge past the reservoir on the right. Through the next field and over another bridge keeping the river to the left until crossing a bridge by the farm and following the path to the Anchor Inn **(B)**.

8. Return along the service road for ³/₄ mile (1.3km) before turning left over a stile opposite Little Scufflings keeping alongside the hedge on the right and over the stiles to the road. For the shortened version continue over the stile opposite and turn left over the stile by the double gates keeping ahead along a water meadow with a fence on the left and stream on the right. At the end of this long meadow go over a bridge beside a picturesque little weir then ahead to a stile and an enclosed green lane to road. Turn right here back into Barcombe and the car park.

   To continue the full walk turn right onto the drive to Banks Farm crossing the road and three more stiles before continuing up a meadow to a bungalow in the top right corner.

9. Cross the stile and go along a path to the road at Mount Pleasant where turn left and in 50 yards (47m) right down the drive to Knowlands Farm.

10. Once past the farm buildings as the track swings off left continue ahead into Knowlands Wood (ignoring the track off right). Immediately before the track passes under the bridge scramble up right onto the old railway track, turning left.

11. Turn left at the crosstracks (just beyond the first telegraph pole on the right) and follow the path across a field, over a stile and along the edge of the playing field behind the school. At the road turn left back to the car park.

POINTS OF INTEREST ON THE WALK

(A) Barcombe Mills

This part of the parish of Barcombe became known as Barcombe Mills because of the group of mills here until their destruction by fire in 1939 (see page 37). The locks have now been adopted as weirs and the navigation a fish ladder owned by the Southern Water Authority. A plaque on the road bridge records the first tollgate in Sussex.

Near Barcombe Mills

(B) Anchor Inn

Built in 1790 it originally catered for bargees until a century later the landlord was caught smuggling and his licence was confiscated. The Inn then became the property of Sir William Grantham of Barcombe Place who carried out several alterations and it was not until 1963 that a licence was renewed. It also has exclusive boating rights along the upstream stretch of the river.

WALK 6 – FOUR HILLS TO KINGSTON

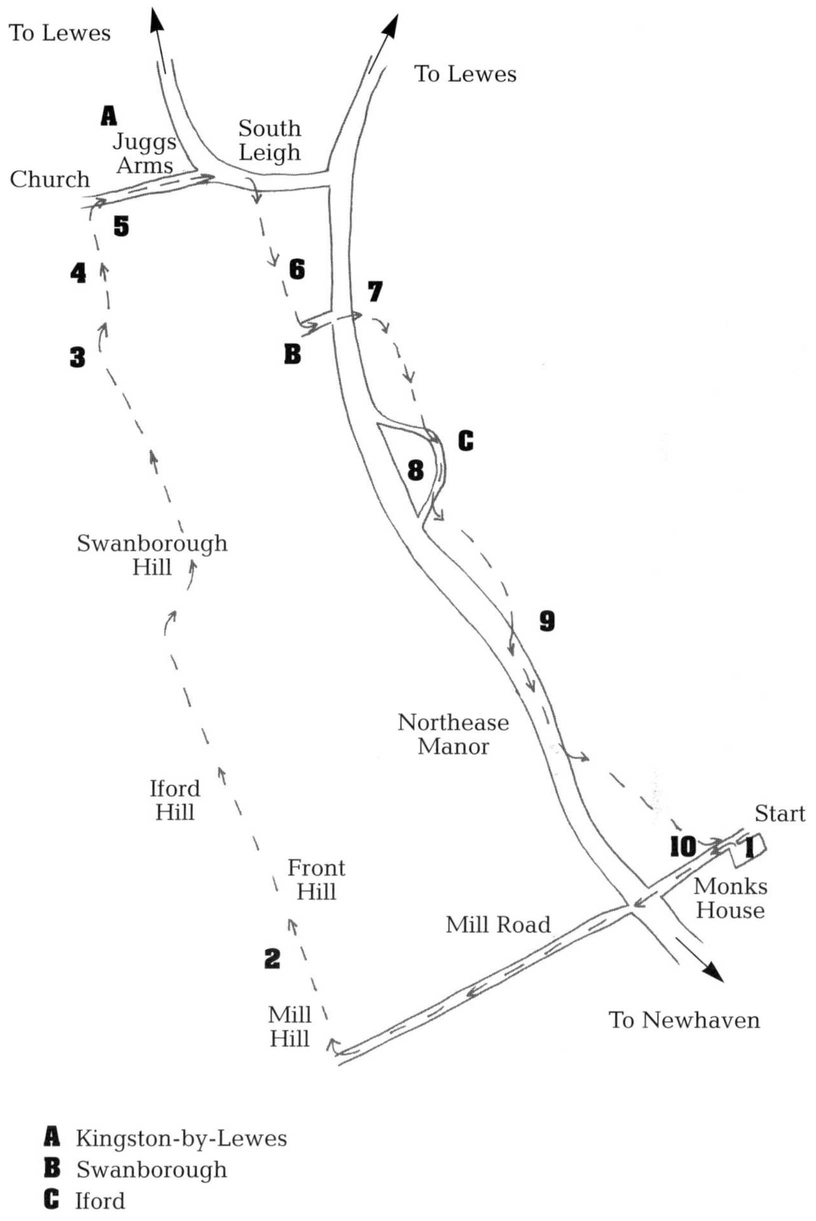

To Lewes

To Lewes

A

Juggs
Arms

South
Leigh

Church

5

4

6

7

3

B

C

8

Swanborough
Hill

9

Iford
Hill

Northease
Manor

Front
Hill

Start

10 **1**

Monks
House

Mill Road

2

To Newhaven

Mill
Hill

A Kingston-by-Lewes
B Swanborough
C Iford

WALK 6 – FOUR HILLS TO KINGSTON

Parking:	Monk's House car park, Rodmell
Map Reference:	Landranger 198 grid reference 421064
Distance:	7¹/₄ miles (11.8km)
Time to Allow:	4 hours
Terrain:	Along the South Downs Way and across the fields in the Ouse valley
Toilets/Refreshments:	Abergavenney Arms, Rodmell Juggs Inn, Kingston
Route:	Rodmell - Mill Hill - Front Hill - Iford Hill - Swanborough Hill - Kingston near Lewes - Swanborough - Iford - Rodmell.

The four hills are along the South Downs Way offering magnificent views across the Ouse valley to Lewes, Mount Caburn and beyond. After the initial ascent of Mill Hill the going is fairly easy until the steep descent into Kingston where extreme caution should be observed. From there on the remainder of the walk is along level ground visiting the village of Kingston, the tiny hamlets of Swanborough and Iford before returning to Rodmell to conclude the walk.

Directions:

1. *Left through the village to the crossroads where cross straight over and up Mill Road where the South Downs Way takes us up to Mill Hill where turn right onto a public bridleway.*
2. *Keep ahead eventually following the concrete track until it turns sharp left where turn right at the acorn marker post then left at the metal gate in 50 yards (47m). This section passes Front Hill and Iford Hill.*
3. *At the marker post opposite the metal gate and cattle grid on the left turn right (but not sharp right) down Swanborough Hill along a track in the direction of the church, turning left almost immediately onto a more obvious track.*
4. *Cross three stiles before turning right onto a track immediately after a fourth stile then cross a fifth stile by a metal gate leading onto the road into Kingston-by-Lewes* **(A)**.
5. *Ahead past the church and Juggs Arms to the T-junction where turn right. In about 250 yards (238m) turn right up a rough track (opposite South Leigh) bearing left in 10 yards (8m) along a footpath by the yellow waymarker.*
6. *Keep ahead through the farm then over a metal stile, bearing left to the road. This is Swanborough* **(B)**.

7. *Cross the road and over the stile bearing right to a gap in the hedge where turn right aross the next field heading in a direction to the right of a small copse ahead. Cross three stiles before turning left at the metalled road into Iford* **(C).**

8. *Follow the road round right turning left over a stile as the road swings off right by "Chaylemore". Cross another stile bearing slightly right across the next field to the road.*

9. *Turn left at the road passing Northease Manor and as the road swings right take the path left across the field to a brick stile in the wall then across a second stile to the road.*

10. *Turn left at the road back to the car park.*

POINTS OF INTEREST ON THE WALK

(A) Kingston-by-Lewes

The church of St Pancras is the first building of note along this lane of flint cottages, with its unusual tapsell gate swinging on its central axis bringing back memories of similar specimens at East Dean, Friston and Jevington. The church dates from the late thirteenth century although three restorations have probably altered the original design. At the end of the lane the Juggs Arms is so called because it stands on the route taken by the Brighton fishwives on their way over the hills to sell their produce in Lewes. They carried their wares in jugs and Juggs Lane along which they travelled still exists en route from Kingston to Lewes.

(B) Swanborough

Mentioned in Domesday Book it boasts a thirteenth century manor house where a court was held until 1860. The late Lady Reading, founder of the Womans Voluntary Service (the Royal came later), lived here and took her place in the House of Lords as Baroness Swanborough.

(C) Iford

Work began on a church here about 1070 and the nave still exists from the original. The present south entrance was opened in a Victorian restoration but the font still stands by the original west entrace. The three pointed arches, now blocked, facing the present entrance were pierced through the Norman north wall to a north aisle in about 1200. This was dismantled following the devastation of the Black Death on the population. The church is still the village's glory built of rough flints like the cottages and wall around it and are all little changed since their induction.

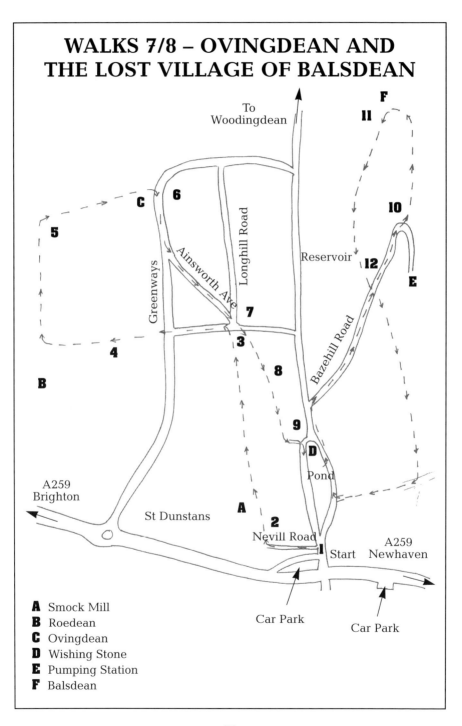

WALKS 7/8 – OVINGDEAN AND THE LOST VILLAGE OF BALSDEAN

To Woodingdean

F

11

C 6

5

Longhill Road

Greenways

Ainsworth Ave

Reservoir

10

12

E

7

3

8

Bazehill Road

4

B

9

D

Pond

A259
Brighton

St Dunstans

A

2

Nevill Road

I

Start

A259
Newhaven

A Smock Mill
B Roedean
C Ovingdean
D Wishing Stone
E Pumping Station
F Balsdean

Car Park

Car Park

WALKS 7/8 – OVINGDEAN AND THE LOST VILLAGE OF BALSDEAN

Parking:	In Rottingdean
Map Reference:	Landranger 198 grid reference 369022
Distance:	3 miles (4.8km) or 5 miles (8km)
Time to Allow:	1½ hours or 2½ hours
Terrain:	Undulating downland and metalled road
Toilets/Refreshments:	In Rottingdean
Route:	Rottingdean – Smock Mill – Beacon Hill – Roedean – Ovingdean – Rottingdean – The Bostle – Balsdean – Rottingdean

Starting from Rottingdean and covering a figure of eight circuit this can quite easily be split into two separate walks or completed in one outing as the mood dictates. The steady climb out of Rottingdean to the mill beside a popular pitch and putt course also provides splendid views back across the channel and once over Beacon Hill there are good views of St Dunstan's home for the blind. A close encounter next with Roedean, the exclusive girl's school, before dropping down on Ovingdean with its delightful church and quaint village atmosphere. Returning to Rottingdean through pleasant woodland the second stage of the walk follows a metalled road to The Bostle before dropping in on the lost village of Balsdean and then back to Rottingdean to complete the figure of eight circuit.

Directions:

1. *Turn up Neville Road continuing along the unmade section and turning right by the blue waymarker beside Beacon House (between Nos. 48 and 50).*

2. *Take the left fork towards the smock mill* **(A)** *keeping ahead by the blue waymarker and ahead again at the crosstracks, continuing to the houses ahead.*

3. *Turn left at the road, crossing Greenways (where there is a good view back left of St Dunstan's) and over the stile continuing up the hill to a second stile in the top right corner of the next field.*

4. *Continue uphill alongside the wire fence on the left, ahead through the old iron gates and ignoring the stile into Roedean* **(B)** *but*

keeping ahead as directed by the yellow waymarkers, over another stile where turn right.

5. Turn right over the stile in the corner of the next field continuing downhill alongside a fence on the left. Pass down some steps beside the churchyard and over a stile right into St Wulfrans, Ovingdean **(C)**.

6. Turn right out of the churchyard and through the village, turning left up Ainsworth Avenue then right into Longhill Road.

7. Take the metalled footpath (signposted Court Ord Road) where, in 15 yards (12m) turn right by the old wooden gatepost taking the left fork almost immediately following this path towards and into the woods.

8. At the large field cross diagonally left to a stile half way along the fence a little way up from the tennis courts. Follow the well defined path alongside the fence on the left, passing through a kissing gate to continue along a path before turning left at the T-junction along a gravel track.

9. On reaching the road turn right back into Rottingdean to complete the initial stage of the walk. To commence the second stage from the pond pass Kipling's House on the left noting the Wishing Stone **(D)** set in the wall. In 100 yards (95m) turn right into Bazehill Road following it up and round left keeping straight ahead once the houses peter out until the Pumping Station **(E)** appears down in the valley to the right.

10. Keep to the left fork as the road continues down the valley to the Pumping Station following this track as it bends round left to the hillocks and trees of the lost village of Balsdean **(F)**.

11. To return turn sharp left up the enclosed track turning left over the isolated stile and keeping to obvious path across next field to another stile keeping alongside fence on the right in the direction of the reservoir ahead.

12. Leave the field by the gate, crossing the road taken on the outward section and through another gate following the blue waymarkers past the backs of some cottages and keeping to the fence on the right to the next gate. Keep ahead along enclosed path to the outskirts of urbanisation on the boundary of Saltdean and Rottingdean where turn right following the track back into Rottingdean.

Smock Windmill, Rottingdean.

POINTS OF INTEREST ON THE WALK

(A) Smock Mill

Erected at its present site in 1812 and although in a very good position for wind it also required constant attention and by 1890 was earmarked for demolition. In 1905/6 the Marquis of Abergavenny (on whose land it stood) had the mill renovated to stem any further decay but by 1922 she was weatherbeaten once more. The Rev. Lewis Verey established a restoration fund purchasing as 99-year lease but it was not until 1935 that enough money was raised to make a complete restoration by which time the mill had lost its patent sweeps, fan and most of its weatherboarding and machinery. The whole of the outer fabric was completely renovated in 1975. This type of mill are known as smock mills simply because they look like a man wearing a smock.

(B) Roedean

The college was completed in 1899 and stands on a site formerly known as Roedean Farm which was purchased in 1895 by the three founding sisters Penelope, Dorothy and Millicent Lawrence. Before this the school – then known as Wimbledon House School – had been established in Kemp Town, but it became so popular that it had outgrown its premises thus necessitating the present location at Roedean.

Roedean School.

(C) Ovingdean (see page 47)

(D) Wishing Stone

Set in the wall of Kipling's House the figure of a face is shrouded in mystery. Legend has it that if the figure's nose is rubbed and the person concerned turns round three times then their wish will come true. Whether Kipling installed the face himself into the wall or whether it was there before his arrival in Rottingdean is unsure but the nose is practically rubbed away suggesting there have been plenty of believers in the legend.

(E) Pumping Station

Built in 1935 at a cost of over £100,000 Balsdean Pumping Station was opened in October the following year by the Mayor of Brighton. Containing two pumps, only one of which operates at any one time, they are capable of drawing up a quarter of a million gallons of water per hour from 200 feet below to the storage reservoir above which, when full, holds 200,000,000 gallons.

(F) Balsdean

Known as Baldesdena in the 12th Century and Ballesden in the 14th Century it became Baldesden then Balsdean and was recognised as a village until its savage destruction by our own militia during the Second World War. Prior to its current identification as one of 38 deserted medieval villages in Sussex it stood proud and desolate in a fold in the hills, a thriving community since the building of its little chapel in 1138 with two farms, a handful of cottages and a handsome manor house. Now there is nothing left save for a few treasured remains that could so easily be overlooked as its entire history was overlooked by those heartless men in Whitehall half a century ago.

The oversite of two buildings can clearly be seen on the right with obvious walled outlines beyond. Round to the right towards the deserted barns is all that remains of the manor house on the left, rebuilt after a fire in 1764, the flint outline of one of the walls barely visible above ground level. A little further on a stone tablet bears an inscription depicting the altar of the Norman chapel desecrated in the latter part of the 18th Century and used as a stable and beyond that a pile of rubble is all that is left of two farm cottages, bulldozed in a heap and left to the elements.

This is a peaceful spot today, silent, eerie almost and yet beautiful in a special tranquillity that only a proud and respectful past can generate.

S.B. Publications publish a wide range of local interest books on Sussex and other parts of the country. For a complete list write to the following address (enclose S.A.E.): c/o 19 Grove Road, Seaford, East Sussex BN25 1TP.